The
AIR FRYER
BIBLE

The AIR FRYER BIBLE

MORE THAN **200** HEALTHIER RECIPES FOR YOUR FAVORITE FOODS

SUSAN LABORDE *and* ELIZABETH HICKMAN

STERLING EPICURE

New York

STERLING EPICURE
New York

An Imprint of Sterling Publishing Co., Inc.
1166 Avenue of the Americas
New York, NY 10036

ISBN 978-1-4549-2707-5

Distributed in Canada by Sterling Publishing Co., Inc.
c/o Canadian Manda Group, 664 Annette Street
Toronto, Ontario, M6S 2C8, Canada
Distributed in the United Kingdom by GMC Distribution Services
Castle Place, 166 High Street, Lewes, East Sussex, BN7 1XU, United Kingdom
Distributed in Australia by NewSouth Books
45 Beach Street, Coogee, NSW 2034, Australia

For information about custom editions,
special sales, and premium and corporate purchases,
please contact Sterling Special Sales at
800-805-5489 or specialsales@sterlingpublishing.com.

Manufactured in Canada

2 4 6 8 10 9 7 5 3

sterlingpublishing.com

Interior design by Gavin Motnyk

A complete list of image credits appears on page 236.

CONTENTS

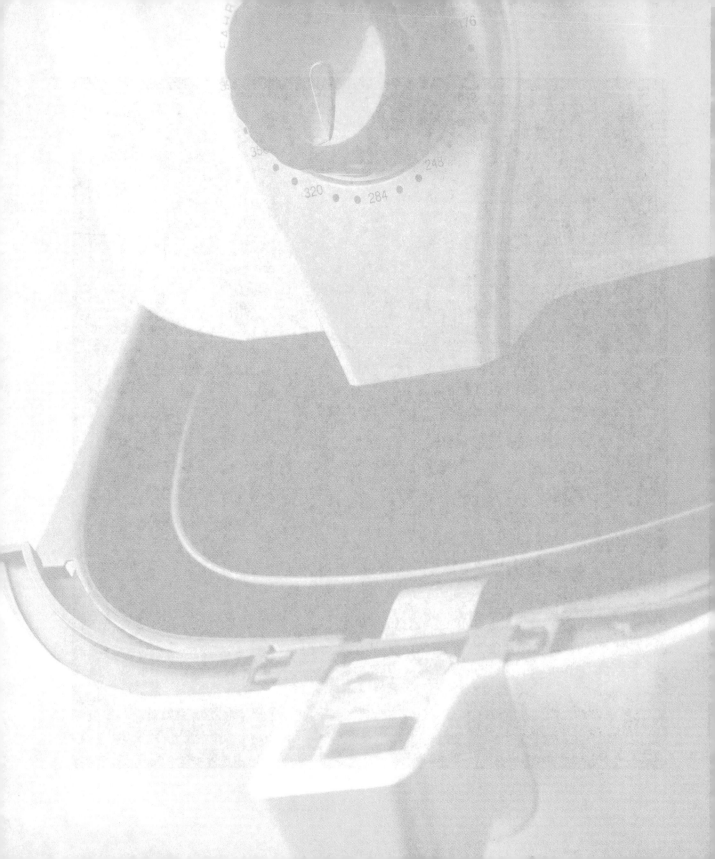

INTRODUCTION

Here in the Deep South, we grew up eating fried everything at every meal. From fried grits for breakfast to fried apple pies for a late-night snack, all our favorite foods were boiled in oil. Our taste buds lived in a grease-happy heaven. Too bad that blissful ignorance couldn't last. As adults, we quickly learned better and grudgingly gave up deep-fried taste for better health.

Then along came the air fryer, an odd-looking appliance promising to produce deep-fried taste without all the grease. We were skeptical. It sounded too good to be true, and you know how that usually works out.

Well, we were in for a shock. Our first attempt resulted in absolutely delicious chicken and French fries. Plus, cleanup was a snap: no more messy grease spatter all over the range and countertop. In no time at all, we were converted.

Once you cook a few basic foods, you'll immediately start wondering what else you can do with your air fryer—and frying with little to no oil is only the beginning. You can use your air fryer to roast, grill, steam, and bake as well. Roasted meats cook faster and taste tender and juicy. Try cooking a pork loin (page 108) or a beef ribeye (page 92). The quality will amaze you. Perhaps most surprising is how beautifully the machine can make baked goods: Banana Bread (page 189), Nutty Whole Wheat Muffins (page 11), Scones (page 197), and Southern Sweet Cornbread (page 198).

The air fryer has become our go-to kitchen gadget. It's fast and convenient, doesn't make a big mess, and is super easy to clean. It works well for a wide range of dishes, from simple to complex, and it's handy for little tasks, such as sautéing a few onions or even, yes, cooking a piece of toast.

We've had great fun developing the recipes for this cookbook—all of them tested one or more times in a home kitchen—which includes everything from easy basics to full meals. Whether you're brand-new to air frying or ready to expand your horizons, we want to welcome you into our kitchen. Come on in and sit awhile. You'll be delighted to discover just how versatile air fryers can be.

Eliminating deep-fried foods is certainly important, but we're concerned about additives, contaminants, and the food supply in general. We want food cooked in a kitchen, not a chemistry lab. Even so, we're pragmatists. In a perfect world, we always would cook from scratch, but spending hours every day on meal prep isn't realistic for most people, including us. So we strive for progress rather than perfection.

For the most part, we avoid fast food and prepackaged foods. We believe in clean eating, and we buy locally grown produce and other foods whenever possible. If you can do that 100 percent of the time, you have our sincere admiration. If not, you'll know that, like ours, sometimes your soul cries out for comfort food, and, healthy or not, it sure makes you feel better. We also admit to having a sweet tooth, as evidenced by our dessert recipes (page 204). Some are light on sugar and other evils; others are guilty pleasures. The good news is that air fryers aren't large enough to handle a twelve-inch pie or three-layer cake. Air fryer desserts give you portion control by default.

Homemade is healthier because you control what goes into your food. You can avoid overprocessed ingredients, GMOs, chemicals, and additives—or you can limit the amounts you consume. That isn't perfect, but it's definitely an improvement!

TIPS FOR AIR FRYER SUCCESS

Know Your Appliance

First, and most important, **read your appliance manual**. All air fryers are not created equal. Features differ among models. Even timers work differently. Parts of some air fryers may be dishwasher safe, but you may have to hand-wash others. Any misuse of your air fryer or its parts could void the warranty. **Read all safety information, and never use the machine in any way that violates the manufacturer's instructions for safe use.** In addition to keeping you safe, your manual should provide details about your model's features and functions. Most of us hate reading instructions or manuals, but it's worth taking the time to understand how to use it. Sometimes that can make all the difference between frustration and success.

Cooking Time

Many factors can affect cooking times, including size, volume, and temperature of food, thickness of breading, and so on. Even your local humidity levels can affect required cooking times. Wattage is another factor. All recipes in this cookbook were tested in 1,425-watt air fryers. A unit with a higher or lower wattage may cook somewhat faster or slower. For most recipes, total cooking time shouldn't vary by more than a minute or two, but to avoid overcooking, check food early and often. Always start with the shortest cooking time listed in a recipe. Check for doneness at that point and continue cooking if necessary. When you try a recipe for the first time and the minimum cooking time is, say, 20 minutes or longer, check the dish at about 15 minutes just to be safe. If you're new to air frying, don't be afraid to pause your air fryer often to open the drawer and check foods. That's the best way to save dinner before it overcooks or burns.

Minimum Temperatures for Food Safety

Consuming raw or undercooked eggs, fish, game, meats, poultry, seafood, or shellfish may increase your risk of foodborne illness. To ensure that foods are safe to eat, ground beef, lamb, pork, and veal should be cooked to a minimum of 160°F. Other cuts of these meats such as beef steaks should be cooked to at least 145°F. All turkey and chicken should be cooked to a minimum of 165°F. Minimum safe temperatures for fish and seafood can vary, and you can find complete information about these foods and more at https://www.food safety.gov/keep/charts/mintemp.html.

Cooking in Batches

For best results, always cut foods into uniform pieces so they cook more evenly. Follow recipes to know whether foods can be stacked or must cook in a single layer. Directions will indicate whether you need to turn or shake the basket to redistribute foods during cooking. All recipes developed for this cookbook were tested in air fryers with an interior capacity of approximately 3 quarts. Using these "standard"-size air fryers often requires cooking in two batches, but many foods cook so quickly that this additional cooking time doesn't matter.

For foods that require lengthy cooking time, the first batch may cool too much while the second batch is cooking, but the solution is simple. Air fryers do an excellent job of reheating foods. Right before your second batch finishes cooking, place your first batch on top so it reheats for serving. If there's not enough room in your air fryer basket, wait until the second batch is done, remove it, and reheat the first batch for a minute or two. Keep this strategy in mind any time you need to heat up leftovers. They come out hot and crispy—unlike microwave-reheated foods, which can feel soggy, rubbery, or tough.

You can also buy a larger air fryer. Some models have a capacity of approximately 5 quarts. If you have an air fryer of this size, you may be able to cook many of our recipes in a single batch. Follow recipe instructions as to whether a particular food can be crowded or stacked, and fill the basket accordingly. You may need to adjust recipe times slightly, but after cooking a few recipes, you'll know how to judge that.

Smoking

Select a suitable location for your unit. If possible, place it near your range so you can use the vent hood if needed. Follow the manufacturer's instructions to protect your countertop and to allow the required amount of open space around the back, sides, and top of your air fryer. Smoking isn't a frequent problem but does occur when cooking meats or other foods with a high fat content. Adding water to the air fryer drawer can help sometimes but not always. Coconut, for example, tends to smoke no matter what. An accumulation of grease in the bottom of your air fryer can also cause smoking. Prevent this problem by keeping the drawer clean and free of food or fat buildup.

Excessive smoking, especially black smoke, is not normal. This could result from an electrical malfunction, in which case unplug your appliance immediately and contact the manufacturer.

TERMS & TECHNIQUES

Using an air fryer isn't complicated, but for most people it's a completely new method of cooking. The information below will help clarify the commonly used terms and techniques in our recipes.

Baking Pan

All baked goods in this cookbook were tested using a 6 x 6 x 3-inch baking pan. You can use any oven-proof dish that fits in your air fryer, but plan ahead. When the food is done, how are you going to remove the dish from the air fryer basket without burning yourself? You can fashion one from folded aluminum foil, but it's easier and safer to buy a pan with a handle. Some pans are rather pricey but well worth the investment so you can enjoy air fryer cooking to the fullest.

Cooking Spray

In addition to Oil for Misting (see page xiii), this is another option for adding a light coating of oil to foods. Cooking sprays are convenient, they nicely prevent food from sticking in your air fryer basket or baking pan, and they're a good choice for misting delicate foods when even extra-light olive oil would add unwanted flavor.

Dredging Station

This assembly line setup makes quick work of breading foods for air fryer cooking. Depending on the recipe, you'll need two or three shallow containers lined up on the counter in the order in which you plan to dip foods. For example, you may have flour in one dish, a beaten egg in a second dish, and breadcrumbs in a third. Proper organization speeds up the coating process. Dredging stations appear in recipes throughout this cookbook, but for convenience we include specific instructions in each recipe.

Food-Grade Gloves

Occasionally our recipes instruct you to mix by hand because that's the best—and sometimes only—way to accomplish certain tasks. You can buy disposable food-grade gloves from restaurant supply stores and numerous vendors online. Poly gloves aren't great because they fit loosely and are less flexible. We prefer powder-free, food-grade vinyl or latex with a snug fit. Gloves are a necessity for handling hot peppers because the oils can cause chemical burns when transferred from bare fingers to eyes.

Muffin Cups

Each recipe indicates which kind of muffin papers to use. With very liquid batters, foil muffin cups hold up better. You may even need to double or triple them. In that case, remove the paper liners, stack two or three foil cups together, and then mist with oil if the recipe requires it. You also can use oven-safe silicone muffin cups, which are sturdy enough to hold most fillings without losing shape while cooking.

Oil for Misting

Most of the time we use a pump-style oil sprayer. It's easy to use and works well whether you need a heavy coating or just a light mist. Refillable oil misters also help reduce the number of cans that end up in landfills. In our misters, we use extra-light olive oil. It has a higher smoke point than extra-virgin olive oil, and it has a very mild taste that won't interfere with other seasonings or overpower the flavor of your foods (except some sweets or very mildly flavored dishes). You can use a pastry brush in a pinch, but we don't recommend it because you'll end up using far more oil than necessary.

INGREDIENTS

These definitions and explanations apply throughout the book.

Breadcrumbs are finely crushed and relatively dry. Sometimes used as filler, they're also commonly used as a coating to produce a light crust. Always use plain, unflavored breadcrumbs unless a recipe specifically calls for a seasoned variety, such as Italian breadcrumbs.

Panko breadcrumbs, sometimes referred to as Japanese style, consist of firmer and bigger flakes than traditional breadcrumbs (above). When you want a coating with lots of crispy crunch, panko is the way to go. Some recipes call for crushed panko because it produces a different texture that tastes better on certain foods. Use a food processor or crush by hand by placing the crumbs in a plastic bag and using a rolling pin or tenderizer.

Butter should be pure sweet cream salted butter, not margarine or imitation spreads.

Cornmeal is available in enriched or whole-grain varieties. We mostly use enriched cornmeal except where specified. You can find stone-ground cornmeal in your local supermarket, farmer's market, or online. As with whole wheat flour, store stone-ground cornmeal in a glass container in the refrigerator.

Cream cheese and **sour cream** can be low fat but not fat free unless the recipe states otherwise. Fat-free cream cheese and sour cream can make a dip or sauce watery and produce other unexpected results. Low fat is a compromise, a healthier choice that still yields a texture similar to the full-fat products.

Flours vary greatly and aren't always interchangeable. In recipes that don't give a specific type, use plain all-purpose white flour. Bleached, unbleached, or all-purpose flour is refined and has had the bran processed out. Manufacturers add nutrients back in to enrich it and compensate for the vitamins and minerals lost in processing. Self-rising flour contains leavening agents to help baked goods rise.

Nineteenth-century cooks prized white flour for its keeping qualities. White-bread loaves kept longer in larders than whole wheat loaves. The same holds true today. White flours have a longer shelf life than whole-grain products and do have their appealing qualities. For high, fluffy biscuits, scones, yeast breads, finely textured cakes, and tender baked goods, only a good white flour will do.

Recipes may use a combination of white flour and whole wheat flour to lighten a dough or batter. Whole wheat flour is healthier of course because it retains the fiber and nutrients of the whole grain. The downside for some uses is that it can result in heavy and dense food. We use two types of whole wheat flour. Most home cooks are familiar with red wheat, which is heartier than enriched flour but can make baked goods heavy and dense—sometimes a good thing. Our favorite whole wheat flour is white wheat. Not the same as white all-purpose flour, it's made from a different strain of wheat and yields a baked good somewhere between a dense, heavy loaf made from red wheat and a light, white flour loaf. You can find white wheat flour at your local market or online. Store whole wheat flours in a glass jar in the refrigerator.

Garlic powder contains only one ingredient: garlic. Do not substitute garlic salt.

Many dried **herbs**, such as dill weed and rosemary, require crushing to release the natural oils. When a recipe calls for crushed herbs, measure the correct amount and then rub the herbs gently between your forefinger and thumb, allowing the herb dust to fall into the bowl or onto the food.

For **crushed ingredients**, how you measure makes a big difference. If a recipe calls for "½ cup crushed [ingredient]," crush it *before* measuring. When a recipe calls for "½ cup [ingredient], crushed," measure first and *then* crush.

Olive oil is our favorite oil because of its health benefits, but when adding oil to a recipe, consider taste. Cold-pressed extra-virgin olive oil has the most distinctive flavor and is an excellent choice when that flavor will enhance the finished dish. For some foods, though, a robust oil can overwhelm the other flavors. For those cases, we use light or extra-light olive oil.

All recipes calling for **milk** were tested using skim / fat-free milk unless the recipe states otherwise.

Pepper always means black pepper, and we use only freshly ground black peppercorns.

Salt always means sea salt.

Yogurt used in recipes may be either Greek or plain unflavored. Compared to regular yogurt, Greek yogurt has less sugar, fewer carbs, and more protein, but it also can have a higher fat content. When a recipe calls for either one, choose according to taste. Greek yogurt has a sharp, tangy flavor that some people don't like, especially in something like a salad dressing that already includes lemon or other pungent flavors.

BREAKFAST & BRUNCH

Apple-Cinnamon-Walnut Muffins

Yield: 8 muffins | Prep Time: 15 minutes | Cooking Time: 9–11 minutes per batch | Total Time: 33–37 minutes

VEGETARIAN

Apples and cinnamon go together beautifully. Add some heart-healthy walnuts for an unbeatable fall combination, but don't be afraid to enjoy these delicious muffins year-round. See insert A1 for recipe photo.

1 cup flour

$\frac{1}{3}$ cup sugar

1 teaspoon baking powder

$\frac{1}{4}$ teaspoon baking soda

$\frac{1}{4}$ teaspoon salt

1 teaspoon cinnamon

$\frac{1}{4}$ teaspoon ginger

$\frac{1}{4}$ teaspoon nutmeg

1 egg

2 tablespoons pancake syrup, plus 2 teaspoons

2 tablespoons melted butter, plus 2 teaspoons

$\frac{3}{4}$ cup unsweetened applesauce

$\frac{1}{2}$ teaspoon vanilla extract

$\frac{1}{4}$ cup chopped walnuts

$\frac{1}{4}$ cup diced apple

8 foil muffin cups, liners removed and sprayed with cooking spray

1. Preheat air fryer to 330°F.

2. In a large bowl, stir together flour, sugar, baking powder, baking soda, salt, cinnamon, ginger, and nutmeg.

3. In a small bowl, beat egg until frothy. Add syrup, butter, applesauce, and vanilla and mix well.

4. Pour egg mixture into dry ingredients and stir just until moistened.

5. Gently stir in nuts and diced apple.

6. Divide batter among the 8 muffin cups.

7. Place 4 muffin cups in air fryer basket and cook at 330°F for 9 to 11 minutes.

8. Repeat with remaining 4 muffins or until toothpick inserted in center comes out clean.

Blueberry Muffins

Yield: 8 muffins | Prep Time: 10 minutes | Cooking Time: 12–14 minutes per batch | Total Time: 34–38 minutes

KID PLEASER   VEGETARIAN

Blueberries are a superfood that's always available because you can buy them frozen year-round. The absolute best muffins are made with freshly picked blueberries and make for a lazy summer breakfast. See insert A1 for recipe photo.

1⅓ cups flour

½ cup sugar

2 teaspoons baking powder

¼ teaspoon salt

⅓ cup canola oil

1 egg

½ cup milk

⅔ cup blueberries, fresh or frozen and thawed

8 foil muffin cups including paper liners

1. Preheat air fryer to 330°F.

2. In a medium bowl, stir together flour, sugar, baking powder, and salt.

3. In a separate bowl, combine oil, egg, and milk and mix well.

4. Add egg mixture to dry ingredients and stir just until moistened.

5. Gently stir in blueberries.

6. Spoon batter evenly into muffin cups.

7. Place 4 muffin cups in air fryer basket and bake at 330°F for 12 to 14 minutes or until tops spring back when touched lightly.

8. Repeat previous step to cook remaining muffins.

Bread Boat Eggs

Yield: 4 servings | Prep Time: 10 minutes | Cooking Time: filling 9–10 minutes, rolls 2–3 minutes | Total Time: 21–23 minutes

VEGETARIAN

Pistolette rolls measure approximately 4 x 2½ inches and are precooked, so they need to bake only long enough to brown. Any brand will do, but we love the light crispiness of Cobblestone pistolettes.

4 pistolette rolls

1 teaspoon butter

¼ cup diced fresh mushrooms

½ teaspoon dried onion flakes

4 eggs

½ teaspoon salt

¼ teaspoon dried dill weed

¼ teaspoon dried parsley

1 tablespoon milk

1. Cut a rectangle in the top of each roll and scoop out center, leaving ½-inch shell on the sides and bottom.

2. Place butter, mushrooms, and dried onion in air fryer baking pan and cook for 1 minute. Stir and cook 3 more minutes.

3. In a medium bowl, beat together the eggs, salt, dill, parsley, and milk. Pour mixture into pan with mushrooms.

4. Cook at 390°F for 2 minutes. Stir. Continue cooking for 3 or 4 minutes, stirring every minute, until eggs are scrambled to your liking.

5. Remove baking pan from air fryer and fill rolls with scrambled egg mixture.

6. Place filled rolls in air fryer basket and cook at 390°F for 2 to 3 minutes or until rolls are lightly browned.

TIP: These rolls also work well when prepared the day before. Follow steps 1 through 5 above, wrap the filled rolls well, and refrigerate overnight. When ready to eat, proceed with step 6. The rolls and filling will be cold, so your reheating time may run slightly longer.

Cheddar-Ham-Corn Muffins

Yield: 8 muffins | Prep Time: 10 minutes | Cooking Time: 6–8 minutes per batch | Total Time: 22–26 minutes

KID PLEASER

For breakfast on the run, grab a couple of these muffins and a piece of fresh fruit, and you're good to go. If you're not in a rush, serve them alongside fruit salad and yogurt. See insert A2 for recipe photo.

¾ cup yellow cornmeal

¼ cup flour

1½ teaspoons baking powder

¼ teaspoon salt

1 egg, beaten

2 tablespoons canola oil

½ cup milk

½ cup shredded sharp Cheddar cheese

½ cup diced ham

8 foil muffin cups, liners removed and sprayed with cooking spray

1. Preheat air fryer to 390°F.

2. In a medium bowl, stir together the cornmeal, flour, baking powder, and salt.

3. Add egg, oil, and milk to dry ingredients and mix well.

4. Stir in shredded cheese and diced ham.

5. Divide batter among the muffin cups.

6. Place 4 filled muffin cups in air fryer basket and bake for 5 minutes.

7. Reduce temperature to 330°F and bake for 1 to 2 minutes or until toothpick inserted in center of muffin comes out clean.

8. Repeat steps 6 and 7 to cook remaining muffins.

Egg Muffins

Yield: 4 servings | Prep Time: 10 minutes | Cooking Time: eggs 8–9 minutes, muffins 3–4 minutes | Total Time: 21–23 minutes

KID PLEASER

This is a fresh alternative to the hockey-puck breakfast sandwiches that you can buy at fast-food joints. It takes a little longer, but peace of mind comes from knowing exactly what you're eating (and what you aren't).

4 eggs

salt and pepper

olive oil

4 English muffins, split

1 cup shredded Colby Jack cheese

4 slices ham or Canadian bacon

1. Preheat air fryer to 390°F.

2. Beat together eggs and add salt and pepper to taste. Spray air fryer baking pan lightly with oil and add eggs. Cook for 2 minutes, stir, and continue cooking for 3 or 4 minutes, stirring every minute, until eggs are scrambled to your preference. Remove pan from air fryer.

3. Place bottom halves of English muffins in air fryer basket. Take half of the shredded cheese and divide it among the muffins. Top each with a slice of ham and one-quarter of the eggs. Sprinkle remaining cheese on top of the eggs. Use a fork to press the cheese into the egg a little so it doesn't slip off before it melts.

4. Cook at 360°F for 1 minute. Add English muffin tops and cook for 2 to 4 minutes to heat through and toast the muffins.

TIP: These will keep in the fridge overnight and taste almost as good as new. After cooking, wrap them tightly or store in a sandwich bag. Reheat in your air fryer just until filling is warm and cheese is melted, and the muffins will have a nice toasty crunch.

French Toast Sticks

Yield: 4 servings | Prep Time: 5 minutes | Cooking Time: 5–7 minutes per batch | Total Time: 15–19 minutes

KID PLEASER   VEGETARIAN

Plain sandwich bread makes these French toast sticks kid-friendly in both size and taste. To make them a little more special, use raisin bread, other specialty breakfast breads, or a nice artisan loaf. See insert A4 for recipe photo.

---

2 eggs

½ cup milk

⅛ teaspoon salt

½ teaspoon pure vanilla extract

¾ cup crushed cornflakes

6 slices sandwich bread, each slice cut into 4 strips

oil for misting or cooking spray

maple syrup or honey

1. In a small bowl, beat together eggs, milk, salt, and vanilla.
2. Place crushed cornflakes on a plate or in a shallow dish.
3. Dip bread strips in egg mixture, shake off excess, and roll in cornflake crumbs.
4. Spray both sides of bread strips with oil.
5. Place bread strips in air fryer basket in single layer.
6. Cook at 390°F for 5 to 7 minutes or until they're dark golden brown.
7. Repeat steps 5 and 6 to cook remaining French toast sticks.
8. Serve with maple syrup or honey for dipping.

VARIATION: For a completely different taste, omit the vanilla and substitute fresh orange juice for the milk. Serve with pineapple spears and orange slices.

Fried PB&J

Yield: 4 servings | Prep Time: 10 minutes | Cooking Time: 6–8 minutes per batch | Total Time: 22–24 minutes

TASTER FAVORITE   VEGETARIAN

This recipe elevates the boring old PB&J to a new level. One of our taste testers doesn't like peanut butter and still thought it was delicious.

½ cup cornflakes, crushed

¼ cup shredded coconut

8 slices oat nut bread or any whole-grain, oversize bread

6 tablespoons peanut butter

2 medium bananas, cut into ½-inch-thick slices

6 tablespoons pineapple preserves

1 egg, beaten

oil for misting or cooking spray

1. Preheat air fryer to 360°F.

2. In a shallow dish, mix together the cornflake crumbs and coconut.

3. For each sandwich, spread one bread slice with 1½ tablespoons of peanut butter. Top with banana slices. Spread another bread slice with 1½ tablespoons of preserves. Combine to make a sandwich.

4. Using a pastry brush, brush top of sandwich lightly with beaten egg. Sprinkle with about 1½ tablespoons of crumb coating, pressing it in to make it stick. Spray with oil.

5. Turn sandwich over and repeat to coat and spray the other side.

6. Cooking 2 at a time, place sandwiches in air fryer basket and cook for 6 to 7 minutes or until coating is golden brown and crispy. If sandwich doesn't brown enough, spray with a little more oil and cook at 390°F for another minute.

7. Cut cooked sandwiches in half and serve warm.

VARIATION: Try apricot or any other mildly flavored preserves.

Hole in One

Yield: 1 serving | Prep Time: 5 minutes | Cooking Time: 6–7 minutes | Total Time: 11–12 minutes

KID PLEASER

The English dish Toad in the Hole consists of sausages baked in a large pan of Yorkshire pudding–style batter. In America, Toad in the Hole is just egg in toast, but our version adds a little extra to make a fast and filling breakfast treat.

1 slice bread

1 teaspoon soft butter

1 egg

salt and pepper

1 tablespoon shredded Cheddar cheese

2 teaspoons diced ham

1. Place a 6 x 6-inch baking dish inside air fryer basket and preheat fryer to 330°F.

2. Using a 2½-inch-diameter biscuit cutter, cut a hole in center of bread slice.

3. Spread softened butter on both sides of bread.

4. Lay bread slice in baking dish and crack egg into the hole. Sprinkle egg with salt and pepper to taste.

5. Cook for 5 minutes.

6. Turn toast over and top it with shredded cheese and diced ham.

7. Cook for 1 to 2 more minutes or until yolk is done to your liking.

> **NOTE:** You can toast the bread circle to serve alongside the finished dish.
>
> **VARIATION:** To make this your own, cook as directed above and add any toppings you enjoy, for example:
> • salsa, sliced tomatoes, and avocadoes
> • chopped apple, dried cranberries, and walnuts
> • Greek yogurt and baby spinach leaves
> • fresh berries, sliced bananas, and a drizzle of honey
> • pizza sauce, pepperoni, and sliced black olives

Not-So-English Muffins

Yield: 4 servings | Prep Time: 5 minutes | Cooking Time: bacon 5–6 minutes, muffins 3–5 minutes | Total Time: 13–16 minutes

The best foods for breakfast are fast, easy, and reasonably healthy. These muffins fit the bill with a flavor combination that offers a nice change of pace from the standard morning fare.

2 strips turkey bacon, cut in half crosswise

2 whole-grain English muffins, split

1 cup fresh baby spinach, long stems removed

¼ ripe pear, peeled and thinly sliced

4 slices Provolone cheese

1. Place bacon strips in air fryer basket and cook for 2 minutes. Check and separate strips if necessary so they cook evenly. Cook for 3 to 4 more minutes, until crispy. Remove and drain on paper towels.

2. Place split muffin halves in air fryer basket and cook at 390°F for 2 minutes, just until lightly browned.

3. Open air fryer and top each muffin with a quarter of the baby spinach, several pear slices, a strip of bacon, and a slice of cheese.

4. Cook at 360°F for 1 to 2 minutes, until cheese completely melts.

Nutty Whole Wheat Muffins

Yield: 8 muffins | Prep Time: 15 minutes | Cooking Time: 9–11 minutes per batch | Total Time: 33–37 minutes

TASTER FAVORITE   VEGETARIAN

Sink your teeth into these hearty muffins for a little bit of sweet and a whole lot of crunch. They're filling enough to stay with you for awhile, which makes them great for breakfast or snacking. See insert A5 for recipe photo.

½ cup whole-wheat flour, plus 2 tablespoons

¼ cup oat bran

2 tablespoons flaxseed meal

¼ cup brown sugar

½ teaspoon baking soda

½ teaspoon baking powder

¼ teaspoon salt

½ teaspoon cinnamon

½ cup buttermilk

2 tablespoons melted butter

1 egg

½ teaspoon pure vanilla extract

½ cup grated carrots

¼ cup chopped pecans

¼ cup chopped walnuts

1 tablespoon pumpkin seeds

1 tablespoon sunflower seeds

16 foil muffin cups, paper liners removed

cooking spray

1. Preheat air fryer to 330°F.

2. In a large bowl, stir together the flour, bran, flaxseed meal, sugar, baking soda, baking powder, salt, and cinnamon.

3. In a medium bowl, beat together the buttermilk, butter, egg, and vanilla. Pour into flour mixture and stir just until dry ingredients moisten. Do not beat.

4. Gently stir in carrots, nuts, and seeds.

5. Double up the foil cups so you have 8 total and spray with cooking spray.

6. Place 4 foil cups in air fryer basket and divide half the batter among them.

7. Cook at 330°F for 9 to 11 minutes or until toothpick inserted in center comes out clean.

8. Repeat step 7 to cook remaining 4 muffins.

Oat Bran Muffins

Yield: 8 muffins | Prep Time: 10 minutes | Cooking Time: 10–12 minutes per batch | Total Time: 30–34 minutes

KID PLEASER   TASTER FAVORITE   VEGETARIAN

Oat bran is high in fiber and a good source of protein and essential nutrients. It also adds delicious taste and texture to baked goods. These muffins are satisfying and substantial and make a great grab-and-go breakfast or snack anytime. See insert A6 for recipe photo.

2/3 cup oat bran

1/2 cup flour

1/4 cup brown sugar

1 teaspoon baking powder

1/2 teaspoon baking soda

1/8 teaspoon salt

1/2 cup buttermilk

1 egg

2 tablespoons canola oil

1/2 cup chopped dates, raisins, or dried cranberries

24 paper muffin cups

cooking spray

1. Preheat air fryer to 330°F.

2. In a large bowl, combine the oat bran, flour, brown sugar, baking powder, baking soda, and salt.

3. In a small bowl, beat together the buttermilk, egg, and oil.

4. Pour buttermilk mixture into bowl with dry ingredients and stir just until moistened. Do not beat.

5. Gently stir in dried fruit.

6. Use triple baking cups to help muffins hold shape during baking. Spray them with cooking spray, place 4 sets of cups in air fryer basket at a time, and fill each one 3/4 full of batter.

7. Cook for 10 to 12 minutes, until top springs back when lightly touched and toothpick inserted in center comes out clean.

8. Repeat for remaining muffins.

Orange Rolls

Yield: 8 rolls | Prep Time: 15 minutes | Cooking Time: 8–10 minutes per batch | Total Time: 31–35 minutes

KID PLEASER   VEGETARIAN

If you have a sweet tooth, you know that every now and then you can't resist indulging it—usually on a lazy Sunday morning. These glazed orange sweet rolls do include some healthy walnuts and dried fruit, but make no mistake: they are decadent.

parchment paper

3 ounces low-fat cream cheese

1 tablespoon low-fat sour cream or plain yogurt (not Greek yogurt)

2 teaspoons sugar

1/4 teaspoon pure vanilla extract

1/4 teaspoon orange extract

1 can (8 count) organic crescent roll dough

1/4 cup chopped walnuts

1/4 cup dried cranberries

1/4 cup shredded, sweetened coconut

butter-flavored cooking spray

Orange Glaze

1/2 cup powdered sugar

1 tablespoon orange juice

1/4 teaspoon orange extract

dash of salt

1. Cut a circular piece of parchment paper slightly smaller than the bottom of your air fryer basket. Set aside.

2. In a small bowl, combine the cream cheese, sour cream or yogurt, sugar, and vanilla and orange extracts. Stir until smooth.

3. Preheat air fryer to 300°F.

4. Separate crescent roll dough into 8 triangles and divide cream cheese mixture among them. Starting at wide end, spread cheese mixture to within 1 inch of point.

5. Sprinkle nuts and cranberries evenly over cheese mixture.

6. Starting at wide end, roll up triangles, then sprinkle with coconut, pressing in lightly to make it stick. Spray tops of rolls with butter-flavored cooking spray.

7. Place parchment paper in air fryer basket, and place 4 rolls on top, spaced evenly.

8. Cook for 8 to 10 minutes, until rolls are golden brown and cooked through.

9. Repeat steps 7 and 8 to cook remaining 4 rolls. You should be able to use the same piece of parchment paper twice.

10. In a small bowl, stir together ingredients for glaze and drizzle over warm rolls.

Pancake Muffins

Yield: 4 servings | Prep Time: 10 minutes | Cooking Time: 7–8 minutes per batch | Total Time: 24–26 minutes

KID PLEASER   VEGETARIAN

Kids love eating muffins that taste like pancakes, especially when they get to choose their favorite fillings. Try some of our suggestions or invent your own!

---

1 cup flour

2 tablespoons sugar (optional)

½ teaspoon baking soda

1 teaspoon baking powder

¼ teaspoon salt

1 egg, beaten

1 cup buttermilk

2 tablespoons melted butter

1 teaspoon pure vanilla extract

24 foil muffin cups

cooking spray

Suggested Fillings

1 teaspoon of jelly or fruit preserves

1 tablespoon or less fresh blueberries; chopped fresh strawberries; chopped frozen cherries; dark chocolate chips; chopped walnuts, pecans, or other nuts; cooked, crumbled bacon or sausage

1. In a large bowl, stir together flour, optional sugar, baking soda, baking powder, and salt.

2. In a small bowl, combine egg, buttermilk, butter, and vanilla. Mix well.

3. Pour egg mixture into dry ingredients and stir to mix well but don't overbeat.

4. Double up the muffin cups and remove the paper liners from the top cups. Spray the foil cups lightly with cooking spray.

5. Place 6 sets of muffin cups in air fryer basket. Pour just enough batter into each cup to cover the bottom. Sprinkle with desired filling. Pour in more batter to cover the filling and fill the cups about ¾ full.

6. Cook at 330°F for 7 to 8 minutes.

7. Repeat steps 5 and 6 for the remaining 6 pancake muffins.

TIP: To make these even faster, use a packaged pancake mix. Look for healthier options, such as Log Cabin All Natural Pancake Mix or Krusteaz Organic Pancake Mix.

Quesadillas

Yield: 4 servings | Prep Time: 10 minutes | Cooking Time: eggs 8–9 minutes,
quesadillas 3 minutes per batch | Total Time: 24–25 minutes

VEGETARIAN

For a spicy wakeup call, have these with hot salsa or Sriracha sauce. For a nice contrast to the heat, serve them hot with cool sliced fruit on the side.

---

4 eggs

2 tablespoons skim milk

salt and pepper

oil for misting or cooking spray

4 flour tortillas

4 tablespoons salsa

2 ounces Cheddar cheese, grated

½ small avocado, peeled and thinly sliced

1. Preheat air fryer to 270°F.

2. Beat together eggs, milk, salt, and pepper.

3. Spray a 6 x 6-inch air fryer baking pan lightly with cooking spray and add egg mixture.

4. Cook 8 to 9 minutes, stirring every 1 to 2 minutes, until eggs are scrambled to your liking. Remove and set aside.

5. Spray one side of each tortilla with oil or cooking spray. Flip over.

6. Divide eggs, salsa, cheese, and avocado among the tortillas, covering only half of each tortilla.

7. Fold each tortilla in half and press down lightly.

8. Place 2 tortillas in air fryer basket and cook at 390°F for 3 minutes or until cheese melts and outside feels slightly crispy. Repeat with remaining two tortillas.

9. Cut each cooked tortilla into halves or thirds.

Quiche Cups

Yield: 10 quiche cups | Prep Time: 15 minutes | Cooking time: sausage 6 minutes,
quiche 9–11 minutes per batch | Total Time: 39–41 minutes

GLUTEN FREE

Most grocery stores offer a good selection of lean sausage that still tastes great. Pork is a favorite option, but some brands made with turkey or chicken also taste good. If you don't like sausage or just want something different, substitute ¼ pound of diced ham. Either version makes an excellent breakfast or brunch treat.

¼ pound all-natural ground pork sausage

3 eggs

¾ cup milk

20 foil muffin cups

cooking spray

4 ounces sharp Cheddar cheese, grated

1. Divide sausage into 3 portions and shape each into a thin patty.

2. Place patties in air fryer basket and cook 390°F for 6 minutes.

3. While sausage is cooking, prepare the egg mixture. A large measuring cup or bowl with a pouring lip works best. Combine the eggs and milk and whisk until well blended. Set aside.

4. When sausage has cooked fully, remove patties from basket, drain well, and use a fork to crumble the meat into small pieces.

5. Double the foil cups into 10 sets. Remove paper liners from the top muffin cups and spray the foil cups lightly with cooking spray.

6. Divide crumbled sausage among the 10 muffin cup sets.

7. Top each with grated cheese, divided evenly among the cups.

8. Place 5 cups in air fryer basket.

9. Pour egg mixture into each cup, filling until each cup is at least ⅔ full.

10. Cook for 8 minutes and test for doneness. A knife inserted into the center shouldn't have any raw egg on it when removed.

11. If needed, cook 1 to 2 more minutes, until egg completely sets.

12. Repeat steps 8 through 11 for the remaining quiches.

Scotch Eggs

Yield: 4 servings | Prep Time: 10 minutes | Cooking Time: 20–25 minutes | Total Time: 30–35 minutes

This recipe eliminates all that grease from deep-fat frying. To lighten it even more, choose ground sausage made from turkey or chicken. See insert A7 for recipe photo.

---

2 tablespoons flour, plus extra for coating

1 pound ground breakfast sausage

4 hardboiled eggs, peeled

1 raw egg

1 tablespoon water

oil for misting or cooking spray

Crumb Coating
¾ cup panko breadcrumbs
¾ cup flour

1. Combine flour with ground sausage and mix thoroughly.

2. Divide into 4 equal portions and mold each around a hardboiled egg so the sausage completely covers the egg.

3. In a small bowl, beat together the raw egg and water.

4. Dip sausage-covered eggs in the remaining flour, then the egg mixture, then roll in the crumb coating.

5. Cook at 360°F for 10 minutes. Spray eggs, turn, and spray other side.

6. Continue cooking for another 10 to 15 minutes or until sausage is well done.

TIP: We recommend Jimmy Dean All-Natural sausage for this recipe.

Spinach-Bacon Rollups

Yield: 4 servings | Prep Time: 5 minutes | Cooking Time: 8–9 minutes | Total Time: 13–14 minutes

SUPER EASY

For a lighter version, substitute whole wheat wraps for the tortillas. If your wraps are extra large, use a bowl or dish as a guide to trim them with a knife or cut them in half before filling.

---

4 flour tortillas (6- or 7-inch size)

4 slices Swiss cheese

1 cup baby spinach leaves

4 slices turkey bacon

1. Preheat air fryer to 390°F.

2. On each tortilla, place one slice of cheese and $\frac{1}{4}$ cup of spinach.

3. Roll up tortillas and wrap each with a strip of bacon. Secure each end with a toothpick.

4. Place rollups in air fryer basket, leaving a little space in between them.

5. Cook for 4 minutes. Turn and rearrange rollups (for more even cooking) and cook for 4 to 5 minutes longer, until bacon is crisp.

> **VARIATION:** Before rolling, add tasty little extras such as strips of roasted red peppers or sundried tomatoes (well drained, patted dry). Also try olives, nuts, or dried fruits. Add anything that sounds good to you as long as it isn't wet or drippy.

Strawberry Toast

Yield: 4 toasts | Prep Time: 10 minutes | Cooking Time: 8 minutes | Total Time: 18 minutes

KID PLEASER   SUPER EASY   VEGETARIAN

For best results, choose a firm bread for this recipe. One of our favorites is ciabatta, but other good choices include brioche or any good whole-grain bread. These little toast triangles quickly and easily perk up an otherwise ordinary breakfast.

4 slices bread, ½-inch thick

butter-flavored cooking spray

1 cup sliced strawberries

1 teaspoon sugar

1. Spray one side of each bread slice with butter-flavored cooking spray. Lay slices sprayed side down.

2. Divide the strawberries among the bread slices.

3. Sprinkle evenly with the sugar and place in the air fryer basket in a single layer.

4. Cook at 390°F for 8 minutes. The bottom should look brown and crisp and the top should look glazed.

TIP: When using firm bread, cutting it into triangles helps it fit in the basket.

Sweet Potato-Cinnamon Toast

Yield: 6–8 slices | Prep Time: 5 minutes | Cooking Time: 8 minutes | Total Time: 13 minutes

GLUTEN FREE   SUPER EASY   VEGETARIAN

Sweet potato can take forever to cook in a toaster, and if you aren't careful it also can make a big mess. It works great in an air fryer, though, and is so versatile. Eat it plain for breakfast, or omit the cinnamon and use it as a base for a quick healthy snack or lunch stack.

---

1 small sweet potato, cut into ⅜-inch slices

oil for misting

ground cinnamon

1. Preheat air fryer to 390°F.

2. Spray both sides of sweet potato slices with oil. Sprinkle both sides with cinnamon to taste.

3. Place potato slices in air fryer basket in a single layer.

4. Cook for 4 minutes, turn, and cook for 4 more minutes or until potato slices are barely fork tender.

VARIATION: Flavor these toast slices any way you like. Instead of cinnamon, try any of your favorite herbs or spices.

Walnut Pancake

Yield: 4 servings | Prep Time: 5 minutes | Cooking Time: 20 minutes | Total Time: 25 minutes

VEGETARIAN

This pancake bakes up tall with a tender, moist middle and a delicious, crunchy crust on top. Best of all, you don't have to stand in front of the range flipping flapjacks for ages.

---

3 tablespoons butter, divided into thirds

1 cup flour

1½ teaspoons baking powder

¼ teaspoon salt

2 tablespoons sugar

¾ cup milk

1 egg, beaten

1 teaspoon pure vanilla extract

½ cup walnuts, roughly chopped

maple syrup or fresh sliced fruit, for serving

1. Place 1 tablespoon of the butter in air fryer baking pan. Cook at 330°F for 3 minutes to melt.

2. In a small dish or pan, melt the remaining 2 tablespoons of butter either in the microwave or on the stove.

3. In a medium bowl, stir together the flour, baking powder, salt, and sugar. Add milk, beaten egg, the 2 tablespoons of melted butter, and vanilla. Stir until combined but do not beat. Batter may be slightly lumpy.

4. Pour batter over the melted butter in air fryer baking pan. Sprinkle nuts evenly over top.

5. Cook for 20 minutes or until toothpick inserted in center comes out clean. Turn air fryer off, close the machine, and let pancake rest for 2 minutes.

6. Remove pancake from pan, slice, and serve with syrup or fresh fruit.

Western Omelet

Yield: 2 servings | Prep Time: 5 minutes | Cooking Time: vegetables 5–6 minutes, omelet 14–16 minutes | Total Time: 24–27 minutes

GLUTEN FREE

This recipe doesn't produce a traditional folded omelet, but you won't mind. It tastes excellent and doesn't demand constant attention while cooking.

¼ cup chopped onion

¼ cup chopped bell pepper, green or red

¼ cup diced ham

1 teaspoon butter

4 large eggs

2 tablespoons milk

⅛ teaspoon salt

¾ cup grated sharp Cheddar cheese

1. Place onion, bell pepper, ham, and butter in air fryer baking pan. Cook at 390°F for 1 minute and stir. Continue cooking 4 to 5 minutes, until vegetables are tender.

2. Beat together eggs, milk, and salt. Pour over vegetables and ham in baking pan. Cook at 360°F for 13 to 15 minutes or until eggs set and top has browned slightly.

3. Sprinkle grated cheese on top of omelet. Cook 1 minute or just long enough to melt the cheese.

APPETIZERS & SNACKS

Apple Rollups

Yield: 8 rollups | Prep Time: 10 minutes | Cooking Time: 4–5 minutes | Total Time: 14–15 minutes

KID PLEASER   SUPER EASY   VEGETARIAN

These rolled grilled cheese sandwiches are great for snacking or as part of a quick lunch.

---

8 slices whole wheat sandwich bread

4 ounces Colby Jack cheese, grated

½ small apple, chopped

2 tablespoons butter, melted

1. Remove crusts from bread and flatten the slices with rolling pin. Don't be gentle. Press hard so that bread will be very thin.

2. Top bread slices with cheese and chopped apple, dividing the ingredients evenly.

3. Roll up each slice tightly and secure each with one or two toothpicks.

4. Brush outside of rolls with melted butter.

5. Place in air fryer basket and cook at 390°F for 4 to 5 minutes, until outside is crisp and nicely browned.

TIP: If, like us, you hate to waste food, freeze the discarded bread crusts and use them later for stuffing or homemade breadcrumbs.

VARIATION: Instead of apple, try finely diced ham. For 8 rollups, you'll need about 3 tablespoons of cubed ham. Both apple and ham together also taste delicious. Just don't overload the bread, or they won't roll easily.

Asian Five-Spice Wings

Yield: 4 servings | Prep Time: 1 hour 10 minutes | Cooking Time: 13–15 minutes | Total Time: 1 hour 23–25 minutes

GLUTEN FREE

These wings don't need dipping sauce. Cook them first, then sprinkle them with five-spice powder. The heat of the wings helps the spice adhere, and this method results in maximum flavor.

2 pounds chicken wings

½ cup Asian-style salad dressing

2 tablespoons Chinese five-spice powder

1. Cut off wing tips and discard or freeze for stock. Cut remaining wing pieces in two at the joint.

2. Place wing pieces in a large sealable plastic bag. Pour in the Asian dressing, seal bag, and massage the marinade into the wings until well coated. Refrigerate for at least an hour.

3. Remove wings from bag, drain off excess marinade, and place wings in air fryer basket.

4. Cook at 360°F for 13 to 15 minutes or until juices run clear. About halfway through cooking time, shake the basket or stir wings for more even cooking.

5. Transfer cooked wings to plate in a single layer. Sprinkle half of the Chinese five-spice powder on the wings, turn, and sprinkle other side with remaining seasoning.

TIP: We recommend using Newman's Own Sesame Ginger Dressing for this recipe.

Asian Rice Logs

Yield: 8 rice logs | Prep Time: 30 minutes | Cooking Time: 5 minutes | Total Time: 35 minutes

VEGETARIAN

You need sticky rice for this recipe. We prefer jasmine, but sushi rice also works well.

1½ cups cooked jasmine or sushi rice

¼ teaspoon salt

2 teaspoons five-spice powder

2 teaspoons diced shallots

1 tablespoon tamari sauce

1 egg, beaten

1 teaspoon sesame oil

2 teaspoons water

⅓ cup plain breadcrumbs

¾ cup panko breadcrumbs

2 tablespoons sesame seeds

Orange Marmalade Dipping Sauce

½ cup all-natural orange marmalade

1 tablespoon soy sauce

1. Make the rice according to package instructions. While the rice is cooking, make the dipping sauce by combining the marmalade and soy sauce and set aside.

2. Stir together the cooked rice, salt, five-spice powder, shallots, and tamari sauce.

3. Divide rice into 8 equal pieces. With slightly damp hands, mold each piece into a log shape. Chill in freezer for 10 to 15 minutes.

4. Mix the egg, sesame oil, and water together in a shallow bowl.

5. Place the plain breadcrumbs on a sheet of wax paper.

6. Mix the panko breadcrumbs with the sesame seeds and place on another sheet of wax paper.

7. Roll the rice logs in plain breadcrumbs, then dip in egg wash, and then dip in the panko and sesame seeds.

8. Cook the logs at 390°F for approximately 5 minutes, until golden brown.

9. Cool slightly before serving with Orange Marmalade Dipping Sauce.

Avocado Fries

Yield: 4 servings | Prep Time: 5 minutes | Cooking Time: 10 minutes | Total Time: 15 minutes

VEGETARIAN

Avocado fries are delicious on their own, but for an extra hit of flavor, dip them in salsa or a ranch-style dressing. See insert C4 for recipe photo.

---

1 egg
1 tablespoon lime juice
1/8 teaspoon hot sauce
2 tablespoons flour
3/4 cup panko breadcrumbs
1/4 cup cornmeal
1/4 teaspoon salt
1 large avocado
oil for misting or cooking spray

1. In a small bowl, whisk together the egg, lime juice, and hot sauce.

2. Place flour on a sheet of wax paper.

3. Mix panko, cornmeal, and salt and place on another sheet of wax paper.

4. Split avocado in half and remove pit. Peel or use a spoon to lift avocado halves from the skin.

5. Cut avocado lengthwise into 1/2-inch slices. Dip each in flour, then egg wash, then roll in panko mixture.

6. Mist with oil or cooking spray and cook at 390°F for 10 minutes, until crust is brown and crispy.

Avocado Fries, Vegan

Yield: 4 servings | Prep Time: 5 minutes | Cooking Time: 10 minutes | Total Time: 15 minutes

VEGETARIAN

These fries make a great choice for snacking because the heart-healthy avocado fills you up and keeps you going. You may also enjoy them for a light, quick lunch on the go.

¼ cup almond or coconut milk

1 tablespoon lime juice

⅛ teaspoon hot sauce

2 tablespoons flour

¾ cup panko breadcrumbs

¼ cup cornmeal

¼ teaspoon salt

1 large avocado

oil for misting or cooking spray

1. In a small bowl, whisk together the almond or coconut milk, lime juice, and hot sauce.

2. Place flour on a sheet of wax paper.

3. Mix panko, cornmeal, and salt and place on another sheet of wax paper.

4. Split avocado in half and remove pit. Peel or use a spoon to lift avocado halves out of the skin.

5. Cut avocado lengthwise into ½-inch slices. Dip each in flour, then milk mixture, then roll in panko mixture.

6. Mist with oil or cooking spray and cook at 390°F for 10 minutes, until crust is brown and crispy.

Bagel Chips

Yield: approx. 2½ cups | Prep Time: 10 minutes | Cooking Time: 2–4 minutes | Total Time: 12–14 minutes

KID PLEASER   SUPER EASY   VEGETARIAN

Making your own bagel chips at home saves money and gives you much better chips than you can buy. The air fryer does the job quickly and eliminates the need for lots of butter. With just a light misting of oil, your chips will toast to perfection. Unlike commercial brands hard enough to break your teeth, these bagel chips have just the right amount of crunch.

Sweet
1 large plain bagel
2 teaspoons sugar
1 teaspoon ground cinnamon
butter-flavored cooking spray

Savory
1 large plain bagel
1 teaspoon Italian seasoning
½ teaspoon garlic powder
oil for misting or cooking spray

1. Preheat air fryer to 390°F.

2. Cut bagel into ¼-inch slices or thinner. (See note below.)

3. Mix the seasonings together.

4. Spread out the slices, mist with oil or cooking spray, and sprinkle with half of the seasonings.

5. Turn over and repeat to coat the other side with oil or cooking spray and seasonings.

6. Place in air fryer basket and cook for 2 minutes. Shake basket or stir a little and continue cooking for 1 to 2 minutes or until toasty brown and crispy.

> **NOTE:** You can slice the bagel into rounds, but that makes it hard to cut slices of uniform thickness. We find it much simpler to lay the bagel flat and slice it height-wise. You end up with chips that vary in dimensions, but it's much easier to cut them all to the same thickness. If you buy unsplit bagels, you can cut them crosswise into rounds. The width of each slice will vary due to the curvature of the bagel, but this difference won't affect cooking.
> **VARIATION:** Try flavored bagels, such as blueberry, cinnamon, or "everything." Because they already contain seasoning, just mist with oil or spray and cook. For sweet bagels, use butter-flavored cooking spray.

Beef Steak Sliders

Yield: 8 sliders | Prep Time: 5 minutes | Cooking Time: steak 12–15 minutes, onions 5–7 minutes | Total Time: 22–27 minutes

TASTER FAVORITE

This hearty snack will please meat lovers. Sirloin is a lean yet flavorful cut of beef, and using light mayonnaise lowers the fat content in the dressing without killing the taste. Try them alongside cool, crunchy carrot sticks.

1 pound top sirloin steaks, about ¾-inch thick

salt and pepper

2 large onions, thinly sliced

1 tablespoon extra-light olive oil

8 slider buns

Horseradish Mayonnaise

1 cup light mayonnaise

4 teaspoons prepared horseradish

2 teaspoons Worcestershire sauce

1 teaspoon coarse brown mustard

1. Place steak in air fryer basket and cook at 390°F for 6 minutes. Turn and cook 5 to 6 more minutes for medium rare. If you prefer your steak medium, continue cooking for 2 to 3 minutes.

2. While the steak is cooking, prepare the Horseradish Mayonnaise by mixing all ingredients together.

3. When steak is cooked, remove from air fryer, sprinkle with salt and pepper to taste, and set aside to rest.

4. Toss the onion slices with the oil and place in air fryer basket. Cook at 390°F for 5 to 7 minutes, until onion rings are soft and browned.

5. Slice steak into very thin slices.

6. Spread slider buns with the horseradish mayo and pile on the meat and onions. Serve with remaining horseradish dressing for dipping.

> **TIP:** For premium taste, buy prime-quality beef, preferably grass fed. If you appreciate the flavor of good steak, it's worth the splurge!

Buffalo Bites

Yield: 16 meatballs | Prep Time: 15 minutes | Cooking Time: 11–12 minutes per batch | Total Time: 37–39 minutes

GLUTEN FREE   TASTER FAVORITE

These tender, juicy balls of ground chicken are bursting with the flavor of traditional hot wings. A cheesy center adds the perfect complement to the hot, spicy meat.

1 pound ground chicken

8 tablespoons buffalo wing sauce

2 ounces Gruyère cheese, cut into 16 cubes

1 tablespoon maple syrup

1. Mix 4 tablespoons buffalo wing sauce into all the ground chicken.

2. Shape chicken into a log and divide into 16 equal portions.

3. With slightly damp hands, mold each chicken portion around a cube of cheese and shape into a firm ball. When you have shaped 8 meatballs, place them in air fryer basket.

4. Cook at 390°F for approximately 5 minutes. Shake basket, reduce temperature to 360°F, and cook for 5 to 6 minutes longer.

5. While the first batch is cooking, shape remaining chicken and cheese into 8 more meatballs.

6. Repeat step 4 to cook second batch of meatballs.

7. In a medium bowl, mix the remaining 4 tablespoons of buffalo wing sauce with the maple syrup. Add all the cooked meatballs and toss to coat.

8. Place meatballs back into air fryer basket and cook at 390°F for 2 to 3 minutes to set the glaze. Skewer each with a toothpick and serve.

TIP: We recommend Frank's RedHot Buffalo Wings Sauce for this recipe.

Cheese Wafers

Yield: 4 dozen | Prep Time: 4 hours 10 minutes | Cooking Time: 5–6 minutes per batch | Total Time: 4 hours 30–34 minutes

KID PLEASER   VEGETARIAN

These freezer-friendly cheese bites make for a quick snack anytime—particularly if you're in the mood for a not-so-guilty pleasure.

---

4 ounces sharp Cheddar cheese, grated

1/4 cup butter

1/2 cup flour

1/4 teaspoon salt

1/2 cup crisp rice cereal

oil for misting or cooking spray

1. Cream the butter and grated cheese together. You can do it by hand, but using a stand mixer is faster and easier.

2. Sift flour and salt together. Add it to the cheese mixture and mix until well blended.

3. Stir in cereal.

4. Place dough on wax paper and shape into a long roll about 1 inch in diameter. Wrap well with the wax paper and chill for at least 4 hours.

5. When ready to cook, preheat air fryer to 360°F.

6. Cut cheese roll into 1/4-inch slices.

7. Spray air fryer basket with oil or cooking spray and place slices in a single layer, close but not touching.

8. Cook for 5 to 6 minutes or until golden brown. When done, place them on paper towels to cool.

9. Repeat previous step to cook remaining cheese bites.

> **TIP:** Follow steps 1 through 4 above, cut the cheese roll into slices, and place the slices on a baking sheet in a single layer. Put the cookie sheet in the freezer for about an hour, then store the raw cheese bites in tightly sealed containers or bags. You can cook these straight from the freezer without needing to thaw them first, and the cooking time will be the same (5 to 6 minutes or until golden brown).

Cinnamon Pita Chips

Yield: 4 servings (32 chips) | Prep Time: 5 minutes | Cooking Time: 4–6 minutes | Total Time: 9–11 minutes

KID PLEASER   SUPER EASY   VEGETARIAN

Making your own pita chips can save a lot of money, especially if you catch a sale on pita bread. This recipe also gives you a great way to use up leftover pita pockets so they don't go stale before you can finish them. For a savory version, see Garlic-Herb Pita Chips (page 45).

---

2 tablespoons sugar

2 teaspoons cinnamon

2 whole 6-inch pitas, whole grain or white

oil for misting or cooking spray

1. Mix sugar and cinnamon together.

2. Cut each pita in half and each half into 4 wedges. Break apart each wedge at the fold.

3. Mist one side of pita wedges with oil or cooking spray. Sprinkle them all with half of the cinnamon sugar.

4. Turn the wedges over, mist the other side with oil or cooking spray, and sprinkle with the remaining cinnamon sugar.

5. Place pita wedges in air fryer basket and cook at 330°F for 2 minutes.

6. Shake basket and cook 2 more minutes. Shake again, and if needed cook 1 or 2 more minutes, until crisp. Watch carefully because at this point they will cook very quickly.

TIP: After cooking, the smooth side will look browner than the rough side. Also, the chips will become a little crispier as they cool.

Corn Dog Muffins

Yield: 8 muffins | Prep Time: 10 minutes | Cooking Time: 8–10 minutes per batch | Total Time: 26–30 minutes

KID PLEASER   TASTER FAVORITE

These corn dogs in a cup can be addictive. They're easy to make, and you can choose much healthier ingredients than the old-fashioned frozen-on-a-stick variety.

1¼ cups sliced kosher hotdogs (3 or 4, depending on size)

½ cup flour

½ cup yellow cornmeal

2 teaspoons baking powder

½ cup skim milk

1 egg

2 tablespoons canola oil

8 foil muffin cups, paper liners removed

cooking spray

mustard or your favorite dipping sauce

1. Slice each hotdog in half lengthwise, then cut in ¼-inch half-moon slices. Set aside.

2. Preheat air fryer to 390°F.

3. In a large bowl, stir together flour, cornmeal, and baking powder.

4. In a small bowl, beat together the milk, egg, and oil until just blended.

5. Pour egg mixture into dry ingredients and stir with a spoon to mix well.

6. Stir in sliced hot dogs.

7. Spray the foil cups lightly with cooking spray.

8. Divide mixture evenly into muffin cups.

9. Place 4 muffin cups in the air fryer basket and cook for 5 minutes.

10. Reduce temperature to 360°F and cook 3 to 5 minutes or until toothpick inserted in center of muffin comes out clean.

11. Repeat steps 9 and 10 to bake remaining corn dog muffins.

12. Serve with mustard or other sauces for dipping.

> **TIP:** We don't add salt to the corn-bread batter because the hot dogs are salty enough for our taste. If you use low-sodium hot dogs, you can add up to ½ teaspoon of salt to the dry ingredients listed above.

Country Wings

Yield: 4+ servings | Prep Time: 1 hour 20 minutes | Cooking Time: 17–19 minutes per batch | Total Time: 1 hour 54–58 minutes

KID PLEASER   TASTER FAVORITE

The perfect combination of outside crunchiness and inside tenderness will make these a hit, especially for anyone who doesn't like overly spicy wings. With these, you get none of the heat but plenty of the good old country-fried chicken flavor.

---

2 pounds chicken wings

Marinade
1 cup buttermilk
½ teaspoon black pepper
½ teaspoon salt

Coating
1 cup flour
1 cup panko breadcrumbs
2 teaspoons salt
2 tablespoons poultry seasoning

oil for misting or cooking spray

1. Cut the tips off the wings. Discard or freeze for stock. Cut remaining wing sections apart at the joint to make 2 pieces per wing. Place wings in a large bowl or plastic bag.

2. Mix together all marinade ingredients and pour over wings. Refrigerate for at least 1 hour but for no more than 8 hours.

3. Preheat air fryer to 360°F.

4. Mix all coating ingredients together in a shallow dish or on wax paper.

5. Remove wings from marinade, shaking off excess, and roll in coating mixture.

6. Spray both sides of each wing with oil or cooking spray.

7. Place wings in air fryer basket in single layer, close but not too crowded. Cook for 17 to 19 minutes or until chicken is done and juices run clear.

8. Repeat step 7 to cook remaining wings.

> **TIP:** The second wing joint cooks faster than the meatier drum joint. Cook the drum joints in one batch and second joints in another. When ready to serve, you can toss the first batch back in the air fryer for a minute to rewarm if needed.

Crab Toasts

Yield: 15–18 toasts | Prep Time: 10 minutes | Cooking Time: 5 minutes per batch | Total Time: 20 minutes

SUPER EASY

Yield may vary depending on the size of the bread you choose. We used whole-grain artisan bread, and the slices measured about 2 x 1½ inches.

---

1 6-ounce can flaked crabmeat, well drained

3 tablespoons light mayonnaise

½ teaspoon lemon juice

1 teaspoon Worcestershire sauce

¼ cup shredded sharp Cheddar cheese

¼ cup shredded Parmesan cheese

1 loaf artisan bread, French bread, or baguette, cut into slices ⅜-inch thick

1. Mix together all ingredients except the bread slices.

2. Spread each slice of bread with a thin layer of crabmeat mixture. (For a bread slice measuring 2 x 1½ inches you will need about ½ tablespoon of crab mixture.)

3. Place in air fryer basket in single layer and cook at 360°F for 5 minutes or until tops brown and toast is crispy.

4. Repeat step 3 to cook remaining crab toasts.

NOTE: Drain the crabmeat very well. If you mix the filling ingredients and liquid collects in the bottom of the bowl, discard it.

TIP: These are a great make-ahead snack for the freezer. Follow steps 1 and 2 above, then place uncooked crab toasts on a cookie sheet and freeze. Store in freezer bags or sealed containers until ready to use. Do not thaw. Place frozen crab toasts in air fryer and cook as directed above, adding about 2 minutes to your total cooking time.

Cuban Sliders

Yield: 8 sliders | Prep Time: 20 minutes | Cooking Time: 8 minutes | Total Time: 28 minutes

SUPER EASY

This is an easy version of the popular Cuban sandwich. The ciabatta toasts up to a nice crunch on the outside, and the add-ons offer a tasty sweet and sharp contrast to the pork.

---

8 slices ciabatta bread, ¼-inch thick

cooking spray

1 tablespoon brown mustard

6-8 ounces thin sliced leftover roast pork

4 ounces thin deli turkey

⅓ cup bread and butter pickle slices

2–3 ounces Pepper Jack cheese slices

1. Spray one side of each slice of bread with butter or olive oil cooking spray.

2. Spread brown mustard on other side of each slice.

3. Layer pork roast, turkey, pickles, and cheese on 4 of the slices. Top with remaining slices.

4. Cook at 390°F for approximately 8 minutes. The sandwiches should be golden brown.

5. Cut each slider in half to make 8 portions.

TIP: If you don't like bread and butter pickles, you can use dill pickle slices or sliced gherkins.

Eggplant Fries

Yield: 4 servings | Prep Time: 10 minutes | Cooking Time: 7–8 minutes per batch | Total Time: 24–26 minutes

TASTER FAVORITE VEGETARIAN

In hot grease, eggplant can act like a sponge. Air frying it, however, affords light and crispy results. See insert B2 for recipe photo.

---

1 medium eggplant

1 teaspoon ground coriander

1 teaspoon cumin

1 teaspoon garlic powder

½ teaspoon salt

1 cup crushed panko breadcrumbs

1 large egg

2 tablespoons water

oil for misting or cooking spray

1. Peel and cut the eggplant into fat fries, ³/₈- to ½-inch thick.

2. Preheat air fryer to 390°F.

3. In a small cup, mix together the coriander, cumin, garlic, and salt.

4. Combine 1 teaspoon of the seasoning mix and panko crumbs in a shallow dish.

5. Place eggplant fries in a large bowl, sprinkle with remaining seasoning, and stir well to combine.

6. Beat eggs and water together and pour over eggplant fries. Stir to coat.

7. Remove eggplant from egg wash, shaking off excess, and roll in panko crumbs.

8. Spray with oil.

9. Place half of the fries in air fryer basket. You should have only a single layer, but it's fine if they overlap a little.

10. Cook for 5 minutes. Shake basket, mist lightly with oil, and cook 2 to 3 minutes longer, until browned and crispy.

11. Repeat step 10 to cook remaining eggplant.

Fried Apple Wedges

Yield: 4 servings | Prep Time: 10 minutes | Cooking Time: 8–9 minutes | Total Time: 18–19 minutes

KID PLEASER VEGETARIAN

You can serve these hot out of the air fryer with a glass of milk for a terrific snack, and they also work as a light dessert.

¼ cup panko breadcrumbs

¼ cup pecans

1½ teaspoons cinnamon

1½ teaspoons brown sugar

¼ cup cornstarch

1 egg white

2 teaspoons water

1 medium apple

oil for misting or cooking spray

1. In a food processor, combine panko, pecans, cinnamon, and brown sugar. Process to make small crumbs.

2. Place cornstarch in a plastic bag or bowl with lid. In a shallow dish, beat together the egg white and water until slightly foamy.

3. Preheat air fryer to 390°F.

4. Cut apple into small wedges. The thickest edge should be no more than ⅜- to ½-inch thick. Cut away the core, but do not peel.

5. Place apple wedges in cornstarch, reseal bag or bowl, and shake to coat.

6. Dip wedges in egg wash, shake off excess, and roll in crumb mixture. Spray with oil.

7. Place apples in air fryer basket in single layer and cook for 5 minutes. Shake basket and break apart any apples that have stuck together. Mist lightly with oil and cook 3 to 4 minutes longer, until crispy.

Fried Bananas

Yield: 4–6 servings | Prep Time: 10 minutes | Cooking Time: 6–8 minutes per batch | Total Time: 22–26 minutes

KID PLEASER   VEGETARIAN

Ripe bananas won't work well for this snack because they fall apart when you try to coat them, so choose firm bananas. If that doesn't sound appealing, don't worry. They will soften during cooking. When you bite into the crispy, nutty coating, you will find a deliciously soft center inside.

½ cup panko breadcrumbs

½ cup sweetened coconut flakes

¼ cup sliced almonds

½ cup cornstarch

2 egg whites

1 tablespoon water

2 firm bananas

oil for misting or cooking spray

1. In food processor, combine panko, coconut, and almonds. Process to make small crumbs.

2. Place cornstarch in a shallow dish. In another shallow dish, beat together the egg whites and water until slightly foamy.

3. Preheat air fryer to 390°F.

4. Cut bananas in half crosswise. Cut each half in quarters lengthwise so you have 16 "sticks."

5. Dip banana sticks in cornstarch and tap to shake off excess. Then dip bananas in egg wash and roll in crumb mixture. Spray with oil.

6. Place bananas in air fryer basket in single layer and cook for 4 minutes. If any spots have not browned, spritz with oil. Cook for 2 to 4 more minutes, until golden brown and crispy.

7. Repeat step 6 to cook remaining bananas.

Fried Green Tomatoes

Yield: 4 servings | Prep Time: 18 minutes | Cooking Time: 10–15 minutes per batch | Total Time: 58–60 minutes

Fried green tomatoes are a summer delight. Drizzle on a bit of horseradish cream and you have a gardener's dream.

---

2 eggs

¼ cup buttermilk

½ cup cornmeal

½ cup breadcrumbs

¼ teaspoon salt

1½ pounds firm green tomatoes,
  cut in ¼-inch slices

oil for misting or cooking spray

Horseradish Drizzle

¼ cup mayonnaise

¼ cup sour cream

2 teaspoons prepared horseradish

½ teaspoon Worcestershire sauce

½ teaspoon lemon juice

⅛ teaspoon black pepper

1. Mix all ingredients for Horseradish Drizzle together and chill while you prepare the green tomatoes.

2. Preheat air fryer to 390°F.

3. Beat the eggs and buttermilk together in a shallow bowl.

4. Mix cornmeal, breadcrumbs, and salt together in a plate or shallow dish.

5. Dip 4 tomato slices in the egg mixture, then roll in the breadcrumb mixture.

6. Mist one side with oil and place in air fryer basket, oil-side down, in a single layer.

7. Mist the top with oil.

8. Cook for 10 to 15 minutes, turning once, until brown and crispy.

9. Repeat steps 5 through 8 to cook remaining tomatoes.

10. Drizzle horseradish sauce over tomatoes just before serving.

TIP: Lay a few Fried Green Tomatoes atop chopped romaine lettuce for a delicious side salad that goes great with grilled steak.

Fried Peaches

Yield: 4 servings | Prep Time: 15 minutes | Cooking Time: 6–8 minutes | Total Time: 21–23 minutes

KID PLEASER   VEGETARIAN

These tasty fruit fries have warm cooked peaches inside and a light crunch outside. They're like eating a mini peach pie.

---

2 egg whites

1 tablespoon water

¼ cup sliced almonds

2 tablespoons brown sugar

½ teaspoon almond extract

1 cup crisp rice cereal

2 medium, very firm peaches, peeled and pitted

¼ cup cornstarch

oil for misting or cooking spray

1. Preheat air fryer to 390°F.

2. Beat together egg whites and water in a shallow dish.

3. In a food processor, combine the almonds, brown sugar, and almond extract. Process until ingredients combine well and the nuts are finely chopped.

4. Add cereal and pulse just until cereal crushes. Pour crumb mixture into a shallow dish or onto a plate.

5. Cut each peach into eighths and place in a plastic bag or container with lid. Add cornstarch, seal, and shake to coat.

6. Remove peach slices from bag or container, tapping them hard to shake off the excess cornstarch. Dip in egg wash and roll in crumbs. Spray with oil.

7. Place in air fryer basket and cook for 5 minutes. Shake basket, separate any that have stuck together, and spritz a little oil on any spots that aren't browning.

8. Cook for 1 to 3 minutes longer, until golden brown and crispy.

> **TIP:** Fresh summer peaches bursting with flavor and dripping with juice won't work well, and so be it. When you're fortunate enough to find those, enjoy them just as they are.

Fried Pickles

Yield: 2 cups | Prep Time: 10 minutes | Cooking Time: 11–15 minutes | Total Time: 21–25 minutes

VEGETARIAN

We first tasted fried pickles long ago at a local catfish restaurant. The air fryer enables us to enjoy a lower-fat version of this yummy treat. See insert B1 for recipe photo.

1 egg

1 tablespoon milk

1/4 teaspoon hot sauce

2 cups sliced dill pickles, well drained

3/4 cup breadcrumbs

oil for misting or cooking spray

1. Preheat air fryer to 390°F.

2. Beat together egg, milk, and hot sauce in a bowl large enough to hold all the pickles.

3. Add pickles to the egg wash and stir well to coat.

4. Place breadcrumbs in a large plastic bag or container with lid.

5. Drain egg wash from pickles and place them in bag with breadcrumbs. Shake to coat.

6. Pile pickles into air fryer basket and spray with oil.

7. Cook for 5 minutes. Shake basket and spray with oil.

8. Cook 5 more minutes. Shake and spray again. Separate any pickles that have stuck together and mist any spots you've missed.

9. Cook for 1 to 5 minutes longer or until dark golden brown and crispy.

Garlic-Herb Pita Chips

Yield: 4 servings (32 chips) | Prep Time: 5 minutes | Cooking Time: 4–6 minutes | Total Time: 9–11 minutes

SUPER EASY   VEGETARIAN

Serve these as a standalone snack, an accompaniment to salads and soups, or with your favorite hummus and dips. For a sweet version, see Cinnamon Pita Chips (page 34).

$\frac{1}{4}$ teaspoon dried basil

$\frac{1}{4}$ teaspoon marjoram

$\frac{1}{4}$ teaspoon ground oregano

$\frac{1}{4}$ teaspoon garlic powder

$\frac{1}{4}$ teaspoon ground thyme

$\frac{1}{4}$ teaspoon salt

2 whole 6-inch pitas, whole grain or white

oil for misting or cooking spray

1. Mix all seasonings together.

2. Cut each pita half into 4 wedges. Break apart wedges at the fold.

3. Mist one side of pita wedges with oil. Sprinkle with half of seasoning mix.

4. Turn pita wedges over, mist the other side with oil, and sprinkle with remaining seasonings.

5. Place pita wedges in air fryer basket and cook at 330°F for 2 minutes.

6. Shake basket and cook for 2 minutes longer. Shake again, and if needed cook for 1 or 2 more minutes, until crisp. Watch carefully because at this point they will cook very quickly.

> **TIP:** After cooking, the smooth side will appear slightly browner than the rough side. Also, the chips will become crispier as they cool.

Garlic Wings

Yield: 4+ servings | Prep Time: 1 hour 20 minutes | Cooking Time: 13–15 minutes per batch | Total Time: 1 hour 33–35 minutes

TASTER FAVORITE

Parmesan cheese is popular with kids of all ages, so don't be surprised at how fast everyone gobbles up these wings!

---

2 pounds chicken wings

oil for misting

cooking spray

Marinade

1 cup buttermilk

2 cloves garlic, mashed flat

1 teaspoon Worcestershire sauce

1 bay leaf

Coating

1½ cups grated Parmesan cheese

¾ cup breadcrumbs

1½ tablespoons garlic powder

½ teaspoon salt

1. Mix all marinade ingredients together.

2. Remove wing tips (the third joint) and discard or freeze for stock. Cut the remaining wings at the joint and toss them into the marinade, stirring to coat well. Refrigerate for at least an hour but no more than 8 hours.

3. When ready to cook, combine all coating ingredients in a shallow dish.

4. Remove wings from marinade, shaking off excess, and roll in coating mixture. Press coating into wings so that it sticks well. Spray wings with oil.

5. Spray air fryer basket with cooking spray. Place wings in basket in single layer, close but not touching.

6. Cook at 360°F for 13 to 15 minutes or until chicken is done and juices run clear.

7. Repeat previous step to cook remaining wings.

> **TIP:** The second wing joint cooks faster than the meatier drum joint. Cook the drum joints in one batch and second joints in another. When ready to serve, you can toss the first batch back in the air fryer for a minute to rewarm if needed.

Granola Three Ways

Yield: 4 cups each recipe | Prep Time: 10 minutes | Cooking Time: 7–10 minutes | Total Time: 17–20 minutes

GLUTEN FREE   VEGETARIAN

Granola makes a great snack for outdoor adventures. You also can use it to make breakfast parfaits by layering it with fresh fruit and plain or flavored yogurt. Fresh peaches are especially tasty with the Blueberry Delight granola and vanilla Greek yogurt. Experiment to discover your favorite combinations.

Nantucket Granola
¼ cup maple syrup
¼ cup dark brown sugar
1 tablespoon butter
1 teaspoon vanilla extract
1 cup rolled oats
½ cup dried cranberries
½ cup walnuts, chopped
¼ cup pumpkin seeds
¼ cup shredded coconut

Blueberry Delight
¼ cup honey
¼ cup light brown sugar
1 tablespoon butter
1 teaspoon lemon extract
1 cup rolled oats

½ cup sliced almonds
½ cup dried blueberries
¼ cup pumpkin seeds
¼ cup sunflower seeds

Cherry Black Forest Mix
¼ cup honey
¼ cup light brown sugar
1 tablespoon butter
1 teaspoon almond extract
1 cup rolled oats
½ cup sliced almonds
½ cup dried cherries
¼ cup shredded coconut
¼ cup dark chocolate chips

oil for misting or cooking spray

1. Combine the syrup or honey, brown sugar, and butter in a small saucepan or microwave-safe bowl. Heat and stir just until butter melts and sugar dissolves. Stir in the extract.

2. Place all other dry ingredients in a large bowl. (For the Cherry Black Forest Mix, don't add the chocolate chips yet.)

3. Pour melted butter mixture over dry ingredients and stir until oat mixture is well coated.

4. Lightly spray a baking pan with oil or cooking spray.

5. Pour granola into pan and cook at 390°F for 5 minutes. Stir. Continue cooking for 2 to 5 minutes, stirring every minute or two, until golden brown. Watch closely. Once the mixture begins to brown, it will cook quickly.

6. Remove granola from pan and spread on wax paper. It will become crispier as it cools.

7. For the Cherry Black Forest Mix, stir in chocolate chips after granola has cooled completely.

8. Store in an airtight container.

> **NOTE:** The cooking method for all three recipes is the same. Simply choose a version and follow the directions.
>
> **TIP:** For a tasty trail mix, make the Cherry Black Forest Mix recipe as above. Once it has cooled completely, stir in up to 1 cup of small pretzels.

Greek Street Tacos

Yield: 8 small tacos | Prep Time: 10 minutes | Cooking Time: 3 minutes | Total Time: 13 minutes

SUPER EASY   VEGETARIAN

This simple and fast recipe makes for a delightful treat that you easily can customize to any individual taste. Start with mini tortillas, use your imagination, and create your own favorite combination of flavors.

8 small flour tortillas (4-inch diameter)

8 tablespoons hummus

4 tablespoons crumbled feta cheese

4 tablespoons chopped kalamata or other olives (optional)

olive oil for misting

1. Place 1 tablespoon of hummus or tapenade in the center of each tortilla. Top with 1 teaspoon of feta crumbles and 1 teaspoon of chopped olives, if using.

2. Using your finger or a small spoon, moisten the edges of the tortilla all around with water.

3. Fold tortilla over to make a half-moon shape. Press center gently. Then press the edges firmly to seal in the filling.

4. Mist both sides with olive oil.

5. Place in air fryer basket very close but try not to overlap.

6. Cook at 390°F for 3 minutes, just until lightly browned and crispy.

TIP: Make sure the tortillas are room temperature so they will fold without cracking. If you need to warm tortillas straight from the fridge, wrap them in damp paper towels and microwave for 30 to 60 seconds, depending on the strength of your microwave, just until they slightly warm and are soft enough to fold without cracking.

Grilled Cheese Sandwich

Yield: 2 sandwiches | Prep Time: 5 minutes | Cooking Time: 5 minutes | Total Time: 10 minutes

KID PLEASER   SUPER EASY   VEGETARIAN

Kids love grilled cheese sandwiches, but they often contain tons of butter and processed cheese. Our recipe uses real Cheddar cheese, and the air fryer eliminates the need for loads of butter. Cutting them into rectangles helps to fit two sandwiches in the air fryer. You can make these with whole-grain bread, but firm white bread makes the best sandwich. Look for a bread made from white wheat.

---

4 slices bread

4 ounces Cheddar cheese slices

2 teaspoons butter or oil

1. Lay the four cheese slices on two of the bread slices and top with the remaining two slices of bread.

2. Brush both sides with butter or oil and cut the sandwiches in rectangular halves.

3. Place in air fryer basket and cook at 390°F for 5 minutes until the outside is crisp and the cheese melts.

Grilled Cheese Sandwich Deluxe

Yield: 4–8 servings | Prep Time: 10 minutes | Cooking Time: 5–6 minutes per batch | Total Time: 20–22 minutes

TASTER FAVORITE   VEGETARIAN

This isn't the grilled cheese you ate as a kid. Each large sandwich makes a hearty meal; half of one of these sandwiches will be plenty for kids and many adults.

8 ounces Brie

8 slices oat nut bread

1 large ripe pear, cored and cut into ½-inch-thick slices

2 tablespoons butter, melted

1. Spread a quarter of the Brie on each of four slices of bread.

2. Top Brie with thick slices of pear, then the remaining 4 slices of bread.

3. Lightly brush both sides of each sandwich with melted butter.

4. Cooking 2 at a time, place sandwiches in air fryer basket and cook at 360°F for 5 to 6 minutes or until cheese melts and outside looks golden brown.

> **TIPS:** If you can't find or don't like oat nut bread, choose any dense whole-grain or artisan bread. The slices should be oversize, the same thickness as ordinary sandwich bread but much larger.

Italian Rice Balls

Yield: 8 rice balls | Prep Time: 20–25 minutes | Cooking Time: 10 minutes | Total Time: 30–35 minutes

VEGETARIAN

The rice used in these balls, also called arancini, should be a sticky type. We like jasmine, but sushi rice also holds together nicely.

1½ cups cooked sticky rice

½ teaspoon Italian seasoning blend

¾ teaspoon salt

8 pitted black olives

1 ounce mozzarella cheese cut into tiny sticks (small enough to stuff into olives)

2 eggs, beaten

⅓ cup Italian breadcrumbs

¾ cup panko breadcrumbs

oil for misting or cooking spray

1. Preheat air fryer to 390°F.

2. Stir together the cooked rice, Italian seasoning, and ½ teaspoon of salt.

3. Stuff each black olive with a piece of mozzarella cheese.

4. Shape the rice into a log and divide into 8 equal pieces. Using slightly damp hands, mold each portion of rice around an olive and shape into a firm ball. Chill in freezer for 10 to 15 minutes or until the outside is cold to the touch.

5. Set up 3 shallow dishes for dipping: beaten eggs in one dish, Italian breadcrumbs in another dish, and in the third dish mix the panko crumbs and remaining salt.

6. Roll each rice ball in breadcrumbs, dip in beaten egg, and then roll in the panko crumbs.

7. Spray all sides with oil.

8. Cook for 10 minutes, until outside is light golden brown and crispy.

VARIATION: These are delicious when eaten plain, but for a jolt of flavor serve them with pizza or spaghetti sauce for dipping.

Jalapeño Poppers

Yield: 18–20 poppers | Prep Time: 60 minutes | Cooking Time: 5 minutes | Total Time: 65 minutes

VEGETARIAN

Make these popular appetizers as mild or as fiery as you like. All the heat of jalapeños lies in the seeds and veins, which you remove before stuffing them. If you like it hot, add some or all of the seeds and veins (chopped) to the filling mixture. Serve with plenty of milk!

½ pound jalapeño peppers

¼ cup cornstarch

1 egg

1 tablespoon lime juice

¼ cup plain breadcrumbs

¼ cup panko breadcrumbs

½ teaspoon salt

oil for misting or cooking spray

Filling

4 ounces cream cheese

1 teaspoon grated lime zest

¼ teaspoon chile powder

⅛ teaspoon garlic powder

¼ teaspoon salt

1. Combine all filling ingredients in small bowl and mix well. Refrigerate while preparing peppers.

2. Cut jalapeños into ½-inch lengthwise slices. Use a small, sharp knife to remove seeds and veins.

   a. For mild appetizers, discard seeds and veins.
   b. For hot appetizers, finely chop seeds and veins. Stir a small amount into filling, taste, and continue adding a little at a time until filling is as hot as you like.

3. Stuff each pepper slice with filling.

4. Place cornstarch in a shallow dish.

5. In another shallow dish, beat together egg and lime juice.

6. Place breadcrumbs and salt in a third shallow dish and stir together.

7. Dip each pepper slice in cornstarch, shake off excess, then dip in egg mixture.

8. Roll in breadcrumbs, pressing to make coating stick.

9. Place pepper slices on a plate in single layer and freeze them for 30 minutes.

10. Preheat air fryer to 390°F.

11. Spray frozen peppers with oil or cooking spray. Place in air fryer basket in a single layer and cook for 5 minutes.

TIP: Don't use low-fat cream cheese for this recipe. Because it's so soft, it's much more likely to melt and leak out before the peppers cook completely. We also highly recommend wearing food-grade gloves while handling the peppers!

Apple-Cinnamon-Walnut Muffins, page 2

Blueberry Muffins, page 3

Cheddar-Ham-Corn Muffins, page 5

Strawberry Pastry Rolls, page 217

French Toast Sticks, page 7

Nutty Whole Wheat Muffins, page 11

Oat Bran Muffins, page 12

Scotch Eggs, page 17

Southern Sweet Cornbread, page 198

Mozzarella Sticks

Yield: 4–8 servings | Prep Time: 10 minutes | Cooking Time: 5 minutes | Total Time: 15 minutes

KID PLEASER   SUPER EASY   VEGETARIAN

Fried cheese always goes well with pizza or marinara sauce, but don't limit your options. Give these cheese sticks a try with ranch dressing; warm apple jelly; barbeque, Sriracha, sweet and sour, teriyaki, or any other sauce you love.

1 egg

1 tablespoon water

8 eggroll wraps

8 mozzarella string cheese "sticks"

sauce for dipping

1. Beat together egg and water in a small bowl.

2. Lay out eggroll wraps and moisten edges with egg wash.

3. Place one piece of string cheese on each wrap near one end.

4. Fold in sides of eggroll wrap over ends of cheese, and then roll up.

5. Brush outside of wrap with egg wash and press gently to seal well.

6. Place in air fryer basket in single layer and cook 390°F for 5 minutes. Cook an additional 1 or 2 minutes, if necessary, until they are golden brown and crispy.

7. Serve with your favorite dipping sauce.

Muffuletta Sliders

Yield: 8 sliders | Prep Time: 10 minutes | Cooking Time: 5–7 minutes per batch | Total Time: 20–24 minutes

TASTER FAVORITE

The authentic New Orleans muffuletta features delicious but decadent piles of salami and mortadella. Our slider version has all those spicy olive flavors but lighter meats. To lower the fat and calories even more, try making it with turkey pastrami.

¼ pound thin-sliced deli ham

¼ pound thin-sliced pastrami

4 ounces low-fat mozzarella cheese, grated or sliced thin

8 slider buns

olive oil for misting

1 tablespoon sesame seeds

Olive Mix

¼ cup sliced black olives

½ cup sliced green olives with pimentos

¼ cup chopped kalamata olives

1 teaspoon red wine vinegar

¼ teaspoon basil

⅛ teaspoon garlic powder

1. In a small bowl, stir together all the Olive Mix ingredients.

2. Divide the meats and cheese into 8 equal portions. To assemble sliders, stack in this order: bottom bun, ham, pastrami, 2 tablespoons olive mix, cheese, top bun.

3. Mist tops of sliders lightly with oil. Sprinkle with sesame seeds.

4. Cooking 4 at a time, place sliders in air fryer basket and cook at 360°F for 5 to 7 minutes to melt cheese and heat through.

> **NOTE:** The Olive Mix also makes a good salad topping. Cut lettuce and tomatoes into small pieces, then combine with the Olive Mix to make a delicious Italian chopped salad.

Potato Chips

Yield: 2–3 servings | Prep Time: 15 minutes | Cooking Time: 15 minutes | Total Time: 30 minutes

GLUTEN FREE   KID PLEASER   SUPER EASY   TASTER FAVORITE   VEGETARIAN

These thin crispy chips will have you giving your mandoline or vegetable parer a workout time and time again. Cutting super-thin slices takes a bit of coordination but is well worth the effort.

---

2 medium potatoes

2 teaspoons extra-light olive oil

oil for misting or cooking spray

salt and pepper

1. Peel the potatoes.

2. Using a mandoline or paring knife, shave potatoes into thin slices, dropping them into a bowl of water as you cut them.

3. Dry potatoes as thoroughly as possible with paper towels or a clean dish towel. Toss potato slices with the oil to coat completely.

4. Spray air fryer basket with cooking spray and add potato slices.

5. Stir and separate with a fork.

6. Cook 390°F for 5 minutes. Stir and separate potato slices. Cook 5 more minutes. Stir and separate potatoes again. Cook another 5 minutes.

7. Season to taste.

> **TIP:** When potato chips have finished cooking, some still will have white centers but crispy outer edges. This is one of the tasty differences that makes these chips so appealing. If you want them all to be brown, remove the browned chips from the basket and continue cooking the others until all the centers are completely brown.

Roasted Chickpeas

Yield: approx. 1 cup | Prep Time: 5 minutes | Cooking Time: 15 minutes | Total Time: 20 minutes

GLUTEN FREE   SUPER EASY   VEGETARIAN

The key to success with this recipe lies in the draining and drying described. Moist chickpeas may not crisp as much as you like. If that happens, don't despair. Cook them a few minutes longer, checking often to make sure they don't burn. See insert B1 for recipe photo.

---

1 15-ounce can chickpeas, drained

2 teaspoons curry powder

¼ teaspoon salt

1 tablespoon olive oil

1. Drain chickpeas thoroughly and spread in a single layer on paper towels. Cover with another paper towel and press gently to remove extra moisture. Don't press too hard or you'll crush the chickpeas.

2. Mix curry powder and salt together.

3. Place chickpeas in a medium bowl and sprinkle with seasonings. Stir well to coat.

4. Add olive oil and stir again to distribute oil.

5. Cook at 390°F for 15 minutes, stopping to shake basket about halfway through cooking time.

6. Cool completely and store in airtight container.

VARIATION: Instead of curry powder, try seasoning with any herbs, spices, or blends that you like, such as garlic, rosemary, Italian seasoning, chile powder, or smoked paprika.

Rumaki

Yield: approx. 24 rumaki | Prep Time: 1 hour 15 minutes |
Cooking Time: 10–12 minutes per batch | Total Time: 1 hour 35–39 minutes

GLUTEN FREE

If you like chicken livers, you'll enjoy this blast from the past and its great blend of flavors and textures. We've lightened it by using turkey bacon, which doesn't hurt the taste. We prefer this recipe to versions that use pork bacon.

10 ounces raw chicken livers

1 can sliced water chestnuts, drained

¼ cup low-sodium teriyaki sauce

12 slices turkey bacon

toothpicks

1. Cut livers into 1½-inch pieces, trimming out tough veins as you slice.

2. Place livers, water chestnuts, and teriyaki sauce in small container with lid. If needed, add another tablespoon of teriyaki sauce to make sure livers are covered. Refrigerate for 1 hour.

3. When ready to cook, cut bacon slices in half crosswise.

4. Wrap 1 piece of liver and 1 slice of water chestnut in each bacon strip. Secure with toothpick.

5. When you have wrapped half of the livers, place them in the air fryer basket in a single layer.

6. Cook at 390°F for 10 to 12 minutes, until liver is done and bacon is crispy.

7. While first batch cooks, wrap the remaining livers. Repeat step 6 to cook your second batch.

Shrimp Pirogues

Yield: 8 servings | Prep Time: 15 minutes | Cooking Time: 4–5 minutes | Total Time: 19–20 minutes

GLUTEN FREE

Early Cajuns traveled the swampy bayous of Louisiana in small boats made from hollowed-out Cypress trees called pirogues, which looked a little like the dugout cucumbers used in these appetizers. Float these little cucumber boats on your next buffet table and watch them disappear.

12 ounces small, peeled, and deveined raw shrimp

3 ounces cream cheese, room temperature

2 tablespoons plain yogurt

1 teaspoon lemon juice

1 teaspoon dried dill weed, crushed

salt

4 small hothouse cucumbers, each approximately 6 inches long

1. Pour 4 tablespoons water in bottom of air fryer drawer.

2. Place shrimp in air fryer basket in single layer and cook at 390°F for 4 to 5 minutes, just until done. Watch carefully because shrimp cooks quickly, and overcooking makes it tough.

3. Chop shrimp into small pieces, no larger than ½ inch. Refrigerate while mixing the remaining ingredients.

4. With a fork, mash and whip the cream cheese until smooth.

5. Stir in the yogurt and beat until smooth. Stir in lemon juice, dill weed, and chopped shrimp.

6. Taste for seasoning. If needed, add ¼ to ½ teaspoon salt to suit your taste.

7. Store in refrigerator until serving time.

8. When ready to serve, wash and dry cucumbers and split them lengthwise. Scoop out the seeds and turn cucumbers upside down on paper towels to drain for 10 minutes.

9. Just before filling, wipe centers of cucumbers dry. Spoon the shrimp mixture into the pirogues and cut in half crosswise. Serve immediately.

TIP: Spread the dilled shrimp mixture on pumpernickel bread for a lovely tea sandwich. It also makes a delicious topping for crackers or toast points.

Spinach Cups

Yield: 30 spinach cups | Prep Time: 15 minutes | Cooking Time: 5 minutes per batch | Total Time: 25 minutes

Serve these warm from the fryer or make them ahead of time and chill. They taste wonderful either way.

1 6-ounce can crabmeat, drained to yield ⅓ cup meat

¼ cup frozen spinach, thawed, drained, and chopped

1 clove garlic, minced

½ cup grated Parmesan cheese

3 tablespoons plain yogurt

¼ teaspoon lemon juice

½ teaspoon Worcestershire sauce

30 mini phyllo shells (2 boxes of 15 each), thawed

cooking spray

1. Remove any bits of shell that might remain in the crabmeat.

2. Mix crabmeat, spinach, garlic, and cheese together.

3. Stir in the yogurt, lemon juice, and Worcestershire sauce and mix well.

4. Spoon a teaspoon of filling into each phyllo shell.

5. Spray air fryer basket and arrange half the shells in the basket.

6. Cook at 390°F for 5 minutes.

7. Repeat with remaining shells.

TIP: These phyllo shells make a great edible container for all kinds of sweet or savory fillings. For a quick one-bite dessert, fill them with lemon curd or pudding and top with a dollop of whipped cream.

String Bean Fries

Yield: 4 servings | Prep Time: 15 minutes | Cooking Time: 5–6 minutes | Total Time: 20–21 minutes

VEGETARIAN

Most people serve string bean fries with ranch dressing for dipping. We like hot creole mustard, but sometimes kids of all ages prefer plain old ketchup. Use your imagination to suit your own taste. See insert B5 for recipe photo.

½ pound fresh string beans

2 eggs

4 teaspoons water

½ cup white flour

½ cup breadcrumbs

¼ teaspoon salt

¼ teaspoon ground black pepper

¼ teaspoon dry mustard (optional)

oil for misting or cooking spray

1. Preheat air fryer to 360°F.

2. Trim stem ends from string beans, wash, and pat dry.

3. In a shallow dish, beat eggs and water together until well blended.

4. Place flour in a second shallow dish.

5. In a third shallow dish, stir together the breadcrumbs, salt, pepper, and dry mustard if using.

6. Dip each string bean in egg mixture, flour, egg mixture again, then breadcrumbs.

7. When you finish coating all the string beans, open air fryer and place them in basket.

8. Cook for 3 minutes.

9. Stop and mist string beans with oil or cooking spray.

10. Cook for 2 to 3 more minutes or until string beans are crispy and nicely browned.

Stuffed Baby Bella Caps

Yield: 16 mushroom caps | Prep Time: 15 minutes | Cooking Time: 12 minutes per batch | Total Time: 39 minutes

TASTER FAVORITE

For best results, use a food processor to make the stuffing. In a pinch, you can mix it in a bowl by hand. It will taste the same, but it won't have the same finely blended texture.

16 fresh, small Baby Bella mushrooms

2 green onions

4 ounces mozzarella cheese

½ cup diced ham

2 tablespoons breadcrumbs

½ teaspoon garlic powder

¼ teaspoon ground oregano

¼ teaspoon ground black pepper

1 to 2 teaspoons olive oil

1. Remove stems and wash mushroom caps.

2. Cut green onions and cheese in small pieces and place in food processor.

3. Add ham, breadcrumbs, garlic powder, oregano, and pepper and mince ingredients.

4. With food processor running, dribble in just enough olive oil to make a thick paste.

5. Divide stuffing among mushroom caps and pack down lightly.

6. Place stuffed mushrooms in air fryer basket in single layer and cook at 390°F for 12 minutes or until tops are golden brown and mushrooms are tender.

7. Repeat step 6 to cook remaining mushrooms.

> **TIP:** For a similar fast and easy dish, see the next recipe, Stuffed Mushrooms (page 62).

Stuffed Mushrooms

Yield: 10–12 mushroom caps | Prep Time: 10 minutes | Cooking Time: 8 minutes | Total Time: 18 minutes

GLUTEN FREE   SUPER EASY   VEGETARIAN

Baby Bella mushrooms work for this recipe, but the white variety will cook faster. When you have more time, try our Stuffed Baby Bella Caps (page 61).

---

8 ounces white mushroom caps, stems removed

salt

6 fresh mozzarella cheese balls

ground dried thyme

¼ roasted red pepper cut into small pieces (about ½ inch)

1. Sprinkle inside of mushroom caps with salt to taste.

2. Cut mozzarella balls in half.

3. Stuff each cap with half a mozzarella cheese ball. Sprinkle very lightly with thyme.

4. Top each mushroom with a small strip of roasted red pepper, lightly pressing it into the cheese.

5. Cook at 390°F for 8 minutes or longer if you prefer softer mushrooms.

TIP: We used mozzarella cheese balls measuring about 1 inch in diameter, which worked well with 2½- to 3-inch mushroom caps. For smaller mushrooms, either use smaller cheese balls or cut the large ones small enough to fit into the caps.

Turkey Bacon Dates

Yield: 16 appetizers | Prep Time: 10 minutes | Cooking Time: 5–7 minutes | Total Time: 15–17 minutes

GLUTEN FREE   SUPER EASY   TASTER FAVORITE

Sometimes eating healthier means sacrificing taste, but not in this case. Turkey bacon cooks exceptionally well in an air fryer, and for these appetizers it tastes better than traditional fatty bacon.

16 whole, pitted dates

16 whole almonds

6 to 8 strips turkey bacon

1. Stuff each date with a whole almond.

2. Depending on the size of your stuffed dates, cut bacon strips into halves or thirds. Each strip should be long enough to wrap completely around a date.

3. Wrap each date in a strip of bacon with ends overlapping and secure with toothpicks.

4. Place in air fryer basket and cook at 390°F for 5 to 7 minutes, until bacon is as crispy as you like.

5. Drain on paper towels or wire rack. Serve hot or at room temperature.

Turkey Burger Sliders

Yield: 8 sliders | Prep Time: 10 minutes | Cooking Time: 5–7 minutes | Total Time: 15–17 minutes

SUPER EASY

The seasonings in the turkey plus the flavors in the toppings give these sliders a uniquely refreshing taste.

1 pound ground turkey

¼ teaspoon curry powder

1 teaspoon Hoisin sauce

½ teaspoon salt

8 slider buns

½ cup slivered red onions

½ cup slivered green or red bell pepper

½ cup fresh chopped pineapple (or pineapple tidbits from kids' fruit cups, drained)

light cream cheese, softened

1. Combine turkey, curry powder, Hoisin sauce, and salt and mix together well.

2. Shape turkey mixture into 8 small patties.

3. Place patties in air fryer basket and cook at 360°F for 5 to 7 minutes, until patties are well done and juices run clear.

4. Place each patty on the bottom half of a slider bun and top with onions, peppers, and pineapple. Spread the remaining bun halves with cream cheese to taste, place on top, and serve.

POULTRY

Buffalo Egg Rolls

Yield: 8 egg rolls | Prep Time: 20 minutes | Cooking Time: 9 minutes per batch | Total Time: 38 minutes

TASTER FAVORITE

Making home-cooked chicken is fast and easy in an air fryer, so we've included a recipe, right. If you prefer, you can use a rotisserie chicken from your grocery store deli, frozen grilled chicken strips, or even leftovers.

1 teaspoon water

1 tablespoon cornstarch

1 egg

2½ cups cooked chicken, diced or shredded (see opposite page)

⅓ cup chopped green onion

⅓ cup diced celery

⅓ cup buffalo wing sauce

8 egg roll wraps

oil for misting or cooking spray

Blue Cheese Dip

3 ounces cream cheese, softened

⅓ cup blue cheese, crumbled

1 teaspoon Worcestershire sauce

¼ teaspoon garlic powder

¼ cup buttermilk (or sour cream)

1. Mix water and cornstarch in a small bowl until dissolved. Add egg, beat well, and set aside.

2. In a medium size bowl, mix together chicken, green onion, celery, and buffalo wing sauce.

3. Divide chicken mixture evenly among 8 egg roll wraps, spooning ½ inch from one edge.

4. Moisten all edges of each wrap with beaten egg wash.

5. Fold the short ends over filling, then roll up tightly and press to seal edges.

6. Brush outside of wraps with egg wash, then spritz with oil or cooking spray.

7. Place 4 egg rolls in air fryer basket.

8. Cook at 390°F for 9 minutes or until outside is brown and crispy.

9. While the rolls are cooking, prepare the Blue Cheese Dip. With a fork, mash together cream cheese and blue cheese.

10. Stir in remaining ingredients.

11. Dip should be just thick enough to slightly cling to egg rolls. If too thick, stir in buttermilk or milk 1 tablespoon at a time until you reach the desired consistency.

12. Cook remaining 4 egg rolls as in steps 7 and 8.

13. Serve while hot with Blue Cheese Dip, more buffalo wing sauce, or both.

TIP: We recommend Frank's RedHot Buffalo Wings Sauce for this recipe.

QUICK CHICKEN FOR FILLING

Yield: 2½ cups | Prep Time: 5 minutes | Cooking Time: 8 minutes | Total Time: 13 minutes

This recipe makes moist, tender chicken intended for use as a filling. Even when fully cooked, it won't appear brown on the outside.

---

1 pound chicken tenders, skinless and boneless

½ teaspoon ground cumin

½ teaspoon garlic powder

cooking spray

1. Sprinkle raw chicken tenders with seasonings.

2. Spray air fryer basket lightly with cooking spray to prevent sticking.

3. Place chicken in air fryer basket in single layer.

4. Cook at 390°F for 4 minutes, turn chicken strips over, and cook for an additional 4 minutes.

5. Test for doneness. Thick tenders may require an additional minute or two.

Buttermilk-Fried Drumsticks

Yield: 2 servings | Prep Time: 10 minutes | Cooking Time: 25 minutes | Total Time: 35 minutes

KID PLEASER

You can easily double this recipe to serve 4 and make in two batches. After your second batch is done, pop the first batch back in the air fryer for a minute or two to reheat. Air fryers do a great job of reheating foods without drying them out or making them tough. See insert B3 for recipe photo.

1 egg

½ cup buttermilk

¾ cup self-rising flour

¾ cup seasoned panko breadcrumbs

1 teaspoon salt

¼ teaspoon ground black pepper (to mix into coating)

4 chicken drumsticks, skin on

oil for misting or cooking spray

1. Beat together egg and buttermilk in shallow dish.

2. In a second shallow dish, combine the flour, panko crumbs, salt, and pepper.

3. Sprinkle chicken legs with additional salt and pepper to taste.

4. Dip legs in buttermilk mixture, then roll in panko mixture, pressing in crumbs to make coating stick. Mist with oil or cooking spray.

5. Spray air fryer basket with cooking spray.

6. Cook drumsticks at 360°F for 10 minutes. Turn pieces over and cook an additional 10 minutes.

7. Turn pieces to check for browning. If you have any white spots that haven't begun to brown, spritz them with oil or cooking spray. Continue cooking for 5 more minutes or until crust is golden brown and juices run clear. Larger, meatier drumsticks will take longer to cook than small ones.

Chicken Chimichangas

Yield: 4 servings | Prep Time: 20 minutes | Cooking Time: 8–10 minutes | Total Time: 28–30 minutes

For this recipe, use room-temperature tortillas. If you keep them refrigerated, wrap them in wet paper towels and microwave for 30 to 60 seconds to warm. They heat up fast, so watch closely.

2 cups cooked chicken, shredded

2 tablespoons chopped green chiles

$\frac{1}{2}$ teaspoon oregano

$\frac{1}{2}$ teaspoon cumin

$\frac{1}{2}$ teaspoon onion powder

$\frac{1}{4}$ teaspoon garlic powder

salt and pepper

8 flour tortillas (6- or 7-inch diameter)

oil for misting or cooking spray

Chimichanga Sauce

2 tablespoons butter

2 tablespoons flour

1 cup chicken broth

$\frac{1}{4}$ cup light sour cream

$\frac{1}{4}$ teaspoon salt

2 ounces Pepper Jack or Monterey Jack cheese, shredded

1. Make the sauce by melting butter in a saucepan over medium-low heat. Stir in flour until smooth and slightly bubbly. Gradually add broth, stirring constantly until smooth. Cook and stir 1 minute, until the mixture slightly thickens. Remove from heat and stir in sour cream and salt. Set aside.

2. In a medium bowl, mix together the chicken, chiles, oregano, cumin, onion powder, garlic, salt, and pepper. Stir in 3 to 4 tablespoons of the sauce, using just enough to make the filling moist but not soupy.

3. Divide filling among the 8 tortillas. Place filling down the center of tortilla, stopping about 1 inch from edges. Fold one side of tortilla over filling, fold the two sides in, and then roll up. Mist all sides with oil or cooking spray.

4. Place chimichangas in air fryer basket seam side down. To fit more into the basket, you can stand them on their sides with the seams against the sides of the basket.

5. Cook at 360°F for 8 to 10 minutes or until heated through and crispy brown outside.

6. Add the shredded cheese to the remaining sauce. Stir over low heat, warming just until the cheese melts. Don't boil or sour cream may curdle.

7. Drizzle the sauce over the chimichangas.

> **TIP:** Personalize these by adding sour cream, salsa, guacamole, shredded lettuce, chopped tomatoes, or black olives.

Chicken Chunks

Yield: 4 servings | Prep Time: 10 minutes | Cooking Time: 8-10 minutes per batch | Total Time: 26-30 minutes

KID PLEASER   TASTER FAVORITE

Once you taste these tender chunks of real chicken with a light crispy coating, you'll never want to eat another frozen ball of processed chicken bits again. Even kids prefer our homemade version, and the air fryer makes them quick and easy.

1 pound chicken tenders cut in large chunks, about 1½ inches

salt and pepper

½ cup cornstarch

2 eggs, beaten

1 cup panko breadcrumbs

oil for misting or cooking spray

1. Season chicken chunks to your liking with salt and pepper.

2. Dip chicken chunks in cornstarch. Then dip in egg and shake off excess. Then roll in panko crumbs to coat well.

3. Spray all sides of chicken chunks with oil or cooking spray.

4. Place chicken in air fryer basket in single layer and cook at 390°F for 5 minutes. Spray with oil, turn chunks over, and spray other side.

5. Cook for an additional 3 to 5 minutes or until chicken juices run clear and outside is golden brown.

6. Repeat steps 4 and 5 to cook remaining chicken.

Chicken Cordon Bleu

Yield: 4 servings | Prep Time: 20 minutes | Cooking Time: 15–20 minutes | Total Time: 35–40 minutes

The name makes it sound daunting, but making this dish is easier than you might think, and it makes for an elegant meal. Serve it with steamed broccoli and a fresh fruit salad.

4 small boneless, skinless chicken breasts

salt and pepper

4 slices deli ham

4 slices deli Swiss cheese (about 3 to 4 inches square)

2 tablespoons olive oil

2 teaspoons marjoram

¼ teaspoon paprika

1. Split each chicken breast horizontally almost in two, leaving one edge intact.

2. Lay breasts open flat and sprinkle with salt and pepper to taste.

3. Place a ham slice on top of each chicken breast.

4. Cut cheese slices in half and place one half atop each breast. Set aside remaining halves of cheese slices.

5. Roll up chicken breasts to enclose cheese and ham and secure with toothpicks.

6. Mix together the olive oil, marjoram, and paprika. Rub all over outsides of chicken breasts.

7. Place chicken in air fryer basket and cook at 360°F for 15 to 20 minutes, until well done and juices run clear.

8. Remove all toothpicks. To avoid burns, place chicken breasts on a plate to remove toothpicks, then immediately return them to the air fryer basket.

9. Place a half cheese slice on top of each chicken breast and cook for a minute or so just to melt cheese.

Chicken Hand Pies

Yield: 8 pies | Prep Time: 30 minutes | Cooking Time: 10 minutes per batch | Total Time: 50 minutes

KID PLEASER   TASTER FAVORITE

These fun-to-eat pies have all the comfort-food taste of chicken potpie plus the homemade goodness of your own healthy ingredients. Refrigerated leftovers will reheat very well in the air fryer.

3/4 cup chicken broth

3/4 cup frozen mixed peas and carrots

1 cup cooked chicken, chopped

1 tablespoon cornstarch

1 tablespoon milk

salt and pepper

1 8-count can organic flaky biscuits

oil for misting or cooking spray

1. In a medium saucepan, bring chicken broth to a boil. Stir in the frozen peas and carrots and cook for 5 minutes over medium heat. Stir in chicken.

2. Mix the cornstarch into the milk until it dissolves. Stir it into the simmering chicken broth mixture and cook just until thickened.

3. Remove from heat, add salt and pepper to taste, and let cool slightly.

4. Lay biscuits out on wax paper. Peel each biscuit apart in the middle to make 2 rounds so you have 16 rounds total. Using your hands or a rolling pin, flatten each biscuit round slightly to make it larger and thinner.

5. Divide chicken filling among 8 of the biscuit rounds. Place remaining biscuit rounds on top and press edges all around. Use the tines of a fork to crimp biscuit edges and make sure they are sealed well.

6. Spray both sides lightly with oil or cooking spray.

7. Cook in a single layer, 4 at a time, at 330°F for 10 minutes or until biscuit dough is cooked through and golden brown.

> **TIP:** Several good brands of organic biscuits are available, and any of them will work. We recommend Annie's brand. Flaky versions are best for this recipe because they are easier to split apart. Otherwise you may need to use a knife to split each biscuit into 2 rounds.

Chicken Nuggets

Yield: 20–24 nuggets | Prep Time: 20 minutes | Cooking Time: 10–14 minutes per batch | Total Time: 40–48 minutes

KID PLEASER

If you or your kids love the taste of fast-food chicken nuggets, this is a *much* healthier option. These homemade nuggets don't take long to make, and doing it yourself means you know they contain only good-quality chicken without any fillers, additives, or other unwanted ingredients. See insert B4 for recipe photo.

---

1 pound boneless, skinless chicken thighs, cut into 1-inch chunks

$3/4$ teaspoon salt

$1/2$ teaspoon black pepper

$1/2$ teaspoon garlic powder

$1/2$ teaspoon onion powder

$1/2$ cup flour

2 eggs, beaten

$1/2$ cup panko breadcrumbs

3 tablespoons plain breadcrumbs

oil for misting or cooking spray

1. In the bowl of a food processor, combine chicken, $1/2$ teaspoon salt, pepper, garlic powder, and onion powder. Process in short pulses until chicken is very finely chopped and well blended.

2. Place flour in one shallow dish and beaten eggs in another. In a third dish or plastic bag, mix together the panko crumbs, plain breadcrumbs, and $1/4$ teaspoon salt.

3. Shape chicken mixture into small nuggets. Dip nuggets in flour, then eggs, then panko crumb mixture.

4. Spray nuggets on both sides with oil or cooking spray and place in air fryer basket in a single layer, close but not overlapping.

5. Cook at 360°F for 10 minutes. Spray with oil and cook 3 to 4 minutes, until chicken is done and coating is golden brown.

6. Repeat step 5 to cook remaining nuggets.

> **TIP:** If your first batch starts to cool off too much, no problem. About 2 or 3 minutes before the second batch is done, toss the first batch into the air fryer on top of them and finish cooking.

Chicken Parmesan

Yield: 4 servings | Prep Time: 15 minutes | Cooking Time: 9–11 minutes | Total Time: 24–26 minutes

Air frying the chicken makes this much lower in fat than traditional versions. To make it even leaner, consider spaghetti squash, spiral-cut vegetables, or a whole-grain pasta with lower net carbs. For marinara sauce, look for all-natural ingredients and no added sugar.

4 chicken tenders

Italian seasoning

salt

¼ cup cornstarch

½ cup Italian salad dressing

¼ cup panko breadcrumbs

¼ cup grated Parmesan cheese, plus more for serving

oil for misting or cooking spray

8 ounces spaghetti, cooked

1 24-ounce jar marinara sauce

1. Pound chicken tenders with meat mallet or rolling pin until about ¼-inch thick.

2. Sprinkle both sides with Italian seasoning and salt to taste.

3. Place cornstarch and salad dressing in 2 separate shallow dishes.

4. In a third shallow dish, mix together the panko crumbs and Parmesan cheese.

5. Dip flattened chicken in cornstarch, then salad dressing. Dip in the panko mixture, pressing into the chicken so the coating sticks well.

6. Spray both sides with oil or cooking spray. Place in air fryer basket in single layer.

7. Cook at 390°F for 5 minutes. Spray with oil again, turning chicken to coat both sides. See tip about turning.

8. Cook for an additional 4 to 6 minutes or until chicken juices run clear and outside is browned.

9. While chicken is cooking, heat marinara sauce and stir into cooked spaghetti.

10. To serve, divide spaghetti with sauce among 4 dinner plates, and top each with a fried chicken tender. Pass additional Parmesan at the table for those who want extra cheese.

TIP: For best results, use a spatula to slide under chicken pieces and turn them gently. They tend to stick a little because of the Parmesan cheese in the coating, but that's what makes them scrumptious!

Chicken Rochambeau

Yield: 4 servings | Prep Time: 15 minutes | Cooking Time: 20 minutes | Total Time: 35 minutes

Different cooks may argue over which is the "correct" sauce for this classic dish, but this simple mushroom version is our favorite. Everything else cooks in the air fryer, which speeds up prep time and saves on cleanup too.

---

1 tablespoon butter

4 chicken tenders, cut in half crosswise

salt and pepper

¼ cup flour

oil for misting

4 slices ham, ¼- to ⅜-inches thick and large enough to cover an English muffin

2 English muffins, split

Sauce

2 tablespoons butter

½ cup chopped green onions

½ cup chopped mushrooms

2 tablespoons flour

1 cup chicken broth

¼ teaspoon garlic powder

1½ teaspoons Worcestershire sauce

1. Place 1 tablespoon of butter in air fryer baking pan and cook at 390°F for 2 minutes to melt.

2. Sprinkle chicken tenders with salt and pepper to taste, then roll in the ¼ cup of flour.

3. Place chicken in baking pan, turning pieces to coat with melted butter.

4. Cook at 390°F for 5 minutes. Turn chicken pieces over, and spray tops lightly with olive oil. Cook 5 minutes longer or until juices run clear. The chicken will not brown.

5. While chicken is cooking, make the sauce: In a medium saucepan, melt the 2 tablespoons of butter.

6. Add onions and mushrooms and sauté until tender, about 3 minutes.

7. Stir in the flour. Gradually add broth, stirring constantly until you have a smooth gravy.

8. Add garlic powder and Worcestershire sauce and simmer on low heat until sauce thickens, about 5 minutes.

9. When chicken is cooked, remove baking pan from air fryer and set aside.

10. Place ham slices directly into air fryer basket and cook at 390°F for 5 minutes or until hot and beginning to sizzle a little. Remove and set aside on top of the chicken for now.

11. Place the English muffin halves in air fryer basket and cook at 390°F for 1 minute.

12. Open air fryer and place a ham slice on top of each English muffin half. Stack 2 pieces of chicken on top of each ham slice. Cook at 390°F for 1 to 2 minutes to heat through.

13. Place each English muffin stack on a serving plate and top with plenty of sauce.

Chicken Schnitzel Dogs

Yield: 4 servings | Prep Time: 15 minutes | Cooking Time: 8–10 minutes | Total Time: 23–25 minutes

KID PLEASER   TASTER FAVORITE

Schnitzel with a twist, these dogs are fun to eat and healthier than your standard hotdog. Crisp veggie chips make a great accompaniment.

½ cup flour

½ teaspoon salt

1 teaspoon marjoram

1 teaspoon dried parsley flakes

½ teaspoon thyme

1 egg

1 teaspoon lemon juice

1 teaspoon water

1 cup breadcrumbs

4 chicken tenders, pounded thin

oil for misting or cooking spray

4 whole-grain hotdog buns

4 slices Gouda cheese

1 small Granny Smith apple, thinly sliced

½ cup shredded Napa cabbage

coleslaw dressing

1. In a shallow dish, mix together the flour, salt, marjoram, parsley, and thyme.

2. In another shallow dish, beat together egg, lemon juice, and water.

3. Place breadcrumbs in a third shallow dish.

4. Cut each of the flattened chicken tenders in half lengthwise.

5. Dip flattened chicken strips in flour mixture, then egg wash. Let excess egg drip off and roll in breadcrumbs. Spray both sides with oil or cooking spray.

6. Cook at 390°F for 5 minutes. Spray with oil, turn over, and spray other side.

7. Cook for 3 to 5 minutes more, until well done and crispy brown.

8. To serve, place 2 schnitzel strips on bottom of each hotdog bun. Top with cheese, sliced apple, and cabbage. Drizzle with coleslaw dressing and top with other half of bun.

Chicken Strips

Yield: 4 or more servings | Prep Time: 40 minutes | Cooking Time: 6–8 minutes per batch | Total Time: 52–56 minutes

GLUTEN FREE   SUPER EASY

You can use these chicken strips whole or cut them into pieces. They taste great in everything from salads to main dishes. They also freeze well, so you can make them ahead of time on weekends and have plenty on hand to thaw for a quick dinner on a busy night. Our basic marinade below is mildly flavored, so the cooked chicken will work for a variety of uses. Experiment with marinade ingredients to suit your tastes. For example, omit the honey to remove any hint of sweetness or add chile powder and cayenne pepper for some spicy heat.

1 pound chicken tenders

Marinade
¼ cup olive oil

2 tablespoons water

2 tablespoons honey

2 tablespoons white vinegar

½ teaspoon salt

½ teaspoon crushed red pepper

1 teaspoon garlic powder

1 teaspoon onion powder

½ teaspoon paprika

1. Combine all marinade ingredients and mix well.

2. Add chicken and stir to coat. Cover tightly and let marinate in refrigerator for 30 minutes.

3. Remove tenders from marinade and place them in a single layer in the air fryer basket.

4. Cook at 390°F for 3 minutes. Turn tenders over and cook for 3 to 5 minutes longer or until chicken is done and juices run clear.

5. Repeat step 4 to cook remaining tenders.

TIP: Some air fryers have an optional grill plate. If you have one, use it for this recipe and your tenders will turn out even better.

Coconut Chicken with Apricot-Ginger Sauce

Yield: 4 servings | Prep Time: 20 minutes | Cooking Time: 7–8 minutes per batch | Total Time: 34–36 minutes

GLUTEN FREE TASTER FAVORITE

Air fryers do a wonderful job of cooking chicken chunks that turn out super moist and tender. Add a crunchy coconut coating and these may well become your new favorite dish. If you're not a big fan of ginger, try these nuggets plain, with honey, or with most any sweet and sour sauce.

1½ pounds boneless, skinless chicken tenders, cut in large chunks (about 1¼ inches)

salt and pepper

½ cup cornstarch

2 eggs

1 tablespoon milk

3 cups shredded coconut (see below)

oil for misting or cooking spray

Apricot-Ginger Sauce

½ cup apricot preserves

2 tablespoons white vinegar

¼ teaspoon ground ginger

¼ teaspoon low-sodium soy sauce

2 teaspoons white or yellow onion, grated or finely minced

> **TIP:** Coconut has a tendency to smoke when cooked, so place your air fryer next to your range and turn on the overhead exhaust vent. Do this *before* you begin cooking, while your air fryer is still cold and safe to handle.
>
> We like sweetened coconut best, but it does contain processed sugar. If you're not a coconut lover, use 1½ cups coconut mixed with 1½ cups plain panko breadcrumbs, which will make the recipe not gluten free.

1. Mix all ingredients for the Apricot-Ginger Sauce well and let sit for flavors to blend while you cook the chicken.

2. Season chicken chunks with salt and pepper to taste.

3. Place cornstarch in a shallow dish.

4. In another shallow dish, beat together eggs and milk.

5. Place coconut in a third shallow dish. (If also using panko breadcrumbs, as suggested below, stir them to mix well.)

6. Spray air fryer basket with oil or cooking spray.

7. Dip each chicken chunk into cornstarch, shake off excess, and dip in egg mixture.

8. Shake off excess egg mixture and roll lightly in coconut or coconut mixture. Spray with oil.

9. Place coated chicken chunks in air fryer basket in a single layer, close together but without sides touching.

10. Cook at 360°F for 4 minutes, stop, and turn chunks over.

11. Cook an additional 3 to 4 minutes or until chicken is done inside and coating is crispy brown.

12. Repeat steps 9 through 11 to cook remaining chicken chunks.

Cornish Hens with Honey-Lime Glaze

Yield: 2–3 servings | Prep Time: 15 minutes | Cooking Time: 25–30 minutes | Total Time: 40–45 minutes

GLUTEN FREE

When you want to cook something different, Cornish hens make a good choice because they're not outrageously expensive. Try these for a stay-at-home date night or any special occasion for two. To complete the meal, serve with simple sides such as brown rice and Brussels Sprouts (page 152). See insert B6 for recipe photo.

---

1 Cornish game hen (1½–2 pounds)

1 tablespoon honey

1 tablespoon lime juice

1 teaspoon poultry seasoning

salt and pepper

cooking spray

1. To split the hen into halves, cut through breast bone and down one side of the backbone.

2. Mix the honey, lime juice, and poultry seasoning together and brush or rub onto all sides of the hen. Season to taste with salt and pepper.

3. Spray air fryer basket with cooking spray and place hen halves in the basket, skin-side down.

4. Cook at 330°F for 25 to 30 minutes. Hen will be done when juices run clear when pierced at leg joint with a fork. Let hen rest for 5 to 10 minutes before cutting.

TIP: We like to spoon brown rice on plates first. Then carefully remove Cornish hen halves from air fryer and flip over on top of rice (skin-side up) so all those delicious juices drip down into the rice.

Fiesta Chicken Plate

Yield: 4 servings | Prep Time: 15 minutes | Cooking Time: 12–15 minutes | Total Time: 27–30 minutes

GLUTEN FREE SUPER EASY

Don't tell your family or dinner guests how simple this is to make. Let them think you spent hours preparing this festive-looking dish.

---

1 pound boneless, skinless chicken breasts
(2 large breasts)

2 tablespoons lime juice

1 teaspoon cumin

½ teaspoon salt

½ cup grated Pepper Jack cheese

1 16-ounce can refried beans

½ cup salsa

2 cups shredded lettuce

1 medium tomato, chopped

2 avocados, peeled and sliced

1 small onion, sliced into thin rings

sour cream

tortilla chips (optional)

1. Split each chicken breast in half lengthwise.

2. Mix lime juice, cumin, and salt together and brush on all surfaces of chicken breasts.

3. Place in air fryer basket and cook at 390°F for 12 to 15 minutes, until well done.

4. Divide the cheese evenly over chicken breasts and cook for an additional minute to melt cheese.

5. While chicken is cooking, heat refried beans on stovetop or in microwave.

6. When ready to serve, divide beans among 4 plates. Place chicken breasts on top of beans and spoon salsa over. Arrange the lettuce, tomatoes, and avocados artfully on each plate and scatter with the onion rings.

7. Pass sour cream at the table and serve with tortilla chips if desired.

> **TIP:** Small or thin chicken breasts cook faster, so you may want to start checking for doneness at about 7 or 8 minutes.

Nacho Chicken Fries

Yield: 4–6 servings | Prep Time: 20 minutes | Cooking Time: 6–7 minutes per batch | Total Time: 32–34 minutes

KID PLEASER

Kids of all ages love nacho cheese—flavored chips. Choose a healthier organic brand, and they make a tasty coating for slim-cut chicken fingers that are tender inside with a nacho-flavored crust.

1 pound chicken tenders

salt

¼ cup flour

2 eggs

¾ cup panko breadcrumbs

¾ cup crushed organic nacho cheese tortilla chips

oil for misting or cooking spray

Seasoning Mix

1 tablespoon chili powder

1 teaspoon ground cumin

½ teaspoon garlic powder

½ teaspoon onion powder

1. Stir together all seasonings in a small cup and set aside.

2. Cut chicken tenders in half crosswise, then cut into strips no wider than about ½ inch.

3. Preheat air fryer to 390°F.

4. Salt chicken to taste. Place strips in large bowl and sprinkle with 1 tablespoon of the seasoning mix. Stir well to distribute seasonings.

5. Add flour to chicken and stir well to coat all sides.

6. Beat eggs together in a shallow dish.

7. In a second shallow dish, combine the panko, crushed chips, and the remaining 2 teaspoons of seasoning mix.

8. Dip chicken strips in eggs, then roll in crumbs. Mist with oil or cooking spray.

9. Chicken strips will cook best if done in two batches. They can be crowded and overlapping a little but not stacked in double or triple layers.

10. Cook for 4 minutes. Shake basket, mist with oil, and cook 2 to 3 more minutes, until chicken juices run clear and outside is crispy.

11. Repeat step 10 to cook remaining chicken fries.

Peachy Chicken Chunks with Cherries

Yield: 4 servings | Prep Time: 8 minutes | Cooking Time: 14–16 minutes | Total Time: 22–24 minutes

GLUTEN FREE   SUPER EASY

The dark, sweet cherries blend well with the peachy goodness of this chicken dish. Serve with a side of couscous and your favorite green veggie.

⅓ cup peach preserves

1 teaspoon ground rosemary

½ teaspoon black pepper

½ teaspoon salt

½ teaspoon marjoram

1 teaspoon light olive oil

1 pound boneless chicken breasts, cut in 1½-inch chunks

oil for misting or cooking spray

10-ounce package frozen unsweetened dark cherries, thawed and drained

1. In a medium bowl, mix together peach preserves, rosemary, pepper, salt, marjoram, and olive oil.

2. Stir in chicken chunks and toss to coat well with the preserve mixture.

3. Spray air fryer basket with oil or cooking spray and lay chicken chunks in basket.

4. Cook at 390°F for 7 minutes. Stir. Cook for 6 to 8 more minutes or until chicken juices run clear.

5. When chicken has cooked through, scatter the cherries over and cook for additional minute to heat cherries.

Peanut Butter-Barbeque Chicken

Yield: 4 servings | Prep Time: 40 minutes | Cooking Time: 20 minutes | Total Time: 1 hour

GLUTEN FREE   TASTER FAVORITE

Tired of the same old chicken you've cooked a hundred times? Surprise your taste buds with this Indian-inspired dish. The flavor combination is unique but not overpowering, so the result tastes different but not bizarre.

1 pound boneless, skinless chicken thighs

salt and pepper

1 large orange

½ cup barbeque sauce

2 tablespoons smooth peanut butter

2 tablespoons chopped peanuts for garnish (optional)

cooking spray

TIP: We recommend Sweet Baby Ray's barbeque sauce for this recipe. Also, when you baste the chicken during cooking, you don't need a thick coating of sauce. If you use too much, it will drip into the bottom of your air fryer. That won't affect the dish, but it makes for messier cleanup later. Use a pastry brush and coat your chicken lightly as you cook it. If you want stronger flavor, add extra sauce at the table.

1. Season chicken with salt and pepper to taste. Place in a shallow dish or plastic bag.
2. Grate orange peel, squeeze orange and reserve 1 tablespoon of juice for the sauce.
3. Pour remaining juice over chicken and marinate for 30 minutes.
4. Mix together the reserved 1 tablespoon of orange juice, barbeque sauce, peanut butter, and 1 teaspoon grated orange peel.
5. Place ¼ cup of sauce mixture in a small bowl for basting. Set remaining sauce aside to serve with cooked chicken.
6. Preheat air fryer to 360°F. Spray basket with nonstick cooking spray.
7. Remove chicken from marinade, letting excess drip off. Place in air fryer basket and cook for 5 minutes. Turn chicken over and cook 5 minutes longer.
8. Brush both sides of chicken lightly with sauce. (See tip.)
9. Cook chicken 5 minutes, then turn thighs one more time, again brushing both sides lightly with sauce. Cook for 5 more minutes or until chicken is done and juices run clear.
10. Serve chicken with remaining sauce on the side and garnish with chopped peanuts if you like.

Pecan Turkey Cutlets

Yield: 4 servings | Prep Time: 10 minutes | Cooking Time: 10–12 minutes per batch | Total Time: 30–34 minutes

TASTER FAVORITE

The key to this dish lies in processing your coating. Follow the directions below and take care not to pulverize the pecans into nut flour. For the best toasty, nutty taste, you want to stop processing while you still have tiny chunks of pecans.

³⁄₄ cup panko breadcrumbs

¹⁄₄ teaspoon salt

¹⁄₄ teaspoon pepper

¹⁄₄ teaspoon dry mustard

¹⁄₄ teaspoon poultry seasoning

¹⁄₂ cup pecans

¹⁄₄ cup cornstarch

1 egg, beaten

1 pound turkey cutlets, ¹⁄₂-inch thick

salt and pepper

oil for misting or cooking spray

1. Place the panko crumbs, ¹⁄₄ teaspoon salt, ¹⁄₄ teaspoon pepper, mustard, and poultry seasoning in food processor. Process until crumbs are finely crushed. Add pecans and process in short pulses just until nuts are finely chopped. Go easy so you don't overdo it!

2. Preheat air fryer to 360°F.

3. Place cornstarch in one shallow dish and beaten egg in another. Transfer coating mixture from food processor into a third shallow dish.

4. Sprinkle turkey cutlets with salt and pepper to taste.

5. Dip cutlets in cornstarch and shake off excess. Then dip in beaten egg and roll in crumbs, pressing to coat well. Spray both sides with oil or cooking spray.

6. Place 2 cutlets in air fryer basket in a single layer and cook for 10 to 12 minutes or until juices run clear.

7. Repeat step 6 to cook remaining cutlets.

NOTE: In order to cook evenly, your turkey cutlets need to be uniform in size. Occasionally you'll get a package with one thick cutlet. If so, either cook that one longer or use a meat mallet or the side of a plate to pound it to the same thickness as your other cutlets.

Poblano Bake

Yield: 4 servings | Prep Time: 15 minutes | Cooking Time: 11 minutes per batch | Total Time: 37 minutes

GLUTEN FREE

Stuffed green bell peppers are standard fare in many households. This south-of-the-border version uses ground turkey and mild poblano peppers for a spicy twist on that familiar dish. If you like it hot, choose a fiery salsa for your topping or pass Sriracha at the table.

2 large poblano peppers (approx. 5½ inches long excluding stem)

¾ pound ground turkey, raw

¾ cup cooked brown rice

1 teaspoon chile powder

½ teaspoon ground cumin

½ teaspoon garlic powder

4 ounces sharp Cheddar cheese, grated

1 8-ounce jar salsa, warmed

1. Slice each pepper in half lengthwise so that you have four wide, flat pepper halves.

2. Remove seeds and membrane and discard. Rinse inside and out.

3. In a large bowl, combine turkey, rice, chile powder, cumin, and garlic powder. Mix well.

4. Divide turkey filling into 4 portions and stuff one into each of the 4 pepper halves. Press lightly to pack down.

5. Place 2 pepper halves in air fryer basket and cook at 390°F for 10 minutes or until turkey is well done.

6. Top each pepper half with ¼ of the grated cheese. Cook 1 more minute or just until cheese melts.

7. Repeat steps 5 and 6 to cook remaining pepper halves.

8. To serve, place each pepper half on a plate and top with ¼ cup warm salsa.

> **TIP:** We recommend Uncle Ben's Natural Whole Grain Instant Brown Rice for this recipe as well as wearing food-grade gloves when handling the peppers.

Southern-Fried Chicken Livers

Yield: 4 servings | Prep Time: 10 minutes | Cooking Time: 10–12 minutes per batch | Total Time: 30–34 minutes

Fried chicken livers used to be a staple in the South. Liver is a good source of iron and other nutrients, but it's also high in cholesterol. When you do want to indulge, air frying is the way to go because it eliminates all the grease and tastes better than deep-fried.

2 eggs

2 tablespoons water

¾ cup flour

1½ cups panko breadcrumbs

½ cup plain breadcrumbs

1 teaspoon salt

½ teaspoon black pepper

20 ounces chicken livers, salted to taste

oil for misting or cooking spray

1. Beat together eggs and water in a shallow dish. Place the flour in a separate shallow dish.

2. In the bowl of a food processor, combine the panko, plain breadcrumbs, salt, and pepper. Process until well mixed and panko crumbs are finely crushed. Place crumbs in a third shallow dish.

3. Dip livers in flour, then egg wash, and then roll in panko mixture to coat well with crumbs.

4. Spray both sides of livers with oil or cooking spray. Cooking in two batches, place livers in air fryer basket in single layer.

5. Cook at 390°F for 7 minutes. Spray livers, turn over, and spray again. Cook for 3 to 5 more minutes, until done inside and coating is golden brown.

6. Repeat to cook remaining livers.

Taquitos

Yield: 12 taquitos | Prep Time: 15 minutes | Cooking Time: 4–6 minutes per batch | Total Time: 23–27 minutes

GLUTEN FREE

On their own, these taquitos make for a hearty snack or light lunch. To turn them into a more substantial meal, add southwest sides such as black beans, Spanish or lime-flavored rice, and a light salad.

---

1 teaspoon butter

2 tablespoons chopped green onions

1 cup cooked chicken, shredded

2 tablespoons chopped green chiles

2 ounces Pepper Jack cheese, shredded

4 tablespoons salsa

½ teaspoon lime juice

¼ teaspoon cumin

½ teaspoon chile powder

⅛ teaspoon garlic powder

12 corn tortillas

oil for misting or cooking spray

1. Melt butter in a saucepan over medium heat. Add green onions and sauté a minute or two, until tender.

2. Remove from heat and stir in the chicken, green chiles, cheese, salsa, lime juice, and seasonings.

3. Preheat air fryer to 390°F.

4. To soften refrigerated tortillas, wrap in damp paper towels and microwave for 30 to 60 seconds, until slightly warmed.

5. Remove one tortilla at a time, keeping others covered with the damp paper towels. Place a heaping tablespoon of filling into tortilla, roll up and secure with toothpick. Spray all sides with oil or cooking spray.

6. Place taquitos in air fryer basket, either in a single layer or stacked. To stack, leave plenty of space between taquitos and alternate the direction of the layers, 4 on the bottom lengthwise, then 4 more on top crosswise.

7. Cook for 4 to 6 minutes or until brown and crispy.

8. Repeat steps 6 and 7 to cook remaining taquitos.

9. Serve hot with guacamole, sour cream, salsa . . . or all three!

Teriyaki Chicken Legs

Yield: 2 servings | Prep Time: 12 minutes | Cooking Time: 18–20 minutes | Total Time: 30–32 minutes

GLUTEN FREE   KID PLEASER   SUPER EASY

You easily can adapt this super-simple recipe to suit your tastes. Try it with hoisin sauce instead of teriyaki or use a hot and spicy barbeque sauce. It's also easy to double the amounts to serve more. Cook in two batches, and just before the second batch is done, toss in the first legs to reheat.

4 tablespoons teriyaki sauce

1 tablespoon orange juice

1 teaspoon smoked paprika

4 chicken legs

cooking spray

1. Mix together the teriyaki sauce, orange juice, and smoked paprika. Brush on all sides of chicken legs.

2. Spray air fryer basket with nonstick cooking spray and place chicken in basket.

3. Cook at 360°F for 6 minutes. Turn and baste with sauce. Cook for 6 more minutes, turn and baste. Cook for 6 to 8 minutes more, until juices run clear when chicken is pierced with a fork.

Turkey Burgers

Yield: 4 servings | Prep Time: 5 minutes | Cooking Time: 10–13 minutes | Total Time: 15–18 minutes

SUPER EASY   TASTER FAVORITE

We like to dress these sandwiches with standard burger fare, but you don't have to follow the rules. Try pineapple slices, baby spinach, fresh cucumber slices, or anything you like. Using fresh ingredients keeps it healthier, and buying produce in season makes it more economical. See insert B7 for recipe photo.

1 pound ground turkey

¼ cup diced red onion

1 tablespoon grilled chicken seasoning

½ teaspoon dried parsley

½ teaspoon salt

4 slices provolone cheese

4 whole-grain sandwich buns

Suggested toppings: lettuce, sliced tomatoes, dill pickles, and mustard

1. Combine the turkey, onion, chicken seasoning, parsley, and salt and mix well.

2. Shape into 4 patties.

3. Cook at 360°F for 9 to 11 minutes or until turkey is well done and juices run clear.

4. Top each burger with a slice of cheese and cook 1 to 2 minutes to melt.

5. Serve on buns with your favorite toppings.

TIP: We recommend McCormick Montreal Chicken seasoning for this recipe.

Turkey-Hummus Wraps

Yield: 4 servings | Prep Time: 10 minutes | Cooking Time: 3–7 minutes per batch | Total Time: 16–24 minutes

SUPER EASY   TASTER FAVORITE

You can make these with flour tortillas, but for a healthier option look for a 100 percent stone-ground whole wheat wrap. It's a very thin flatbread that is low in calories and high in fiber.

4 large whole wheat wraps

½ cup hummus

16 thin slices deli turkey

8 slices provolone cheese

1 cup fresh baby spinach (or more to taste)

1. To assemble, place 2 tablespoons of hummus on each wrap and spread to within about a half inch from edges. Top with 4 slices of turkey and 2 slices of provolone. Finish with ¼ cup of baby spinach—or pile on as much as you like.

2. Roll up each wrap. You don't need to fold or seal the ends.

3. Place 2 wraps in air fryer basket, seam side down.

4. Cook at 360°F for 3 to 4 minutes to warm filling and melt cheese. If you like, you can continue cooking for 2 or 3 more minutes, until the wrap is slightly crispy.

5. Repeat step 4 to cook remaining wraps.

TIP: Depending on the size of your air fryer basket and the size of your wraps, you may be able to cook all 4 wraps at once. (The more spinach you add, the fatter your rolls will be.) Place 2 wraps in the basket and then stack the other two on top, perpendicular.

Beef, Pork, Lamb & Game

Boneless Ribeyes

Yield: 2–4 servings | Prep Time: 35 minutes | Cooking Time: 10–12 minutes | Total Time: 45–47 minutes

GLUTEN FREE   SUPER EASY   TASTER FAVORITE

If you think air-fried steak sounds like a waste of good meat, you're in for a surprise. Excess fat drains during cooking, and the steak turns out tender, juicy, and delicious. We prefer it to steak cooked by any other indoor method. The total cooking times listed above are approximate, and some air fryers cook faster than others. Watch carefully so that you don't overcook your steaks. See insert B5 for recipe photo.

---

2 8-ounce boneless ribeye steaks

4 teaspoons Worcestershire sauce

1/2 teaspoon garlic powder

pepper

4 teaspoons extra virgin olive oil

salt

1. Season steaks on both sides with Worcestershire sauce. Use the back of a spoon to spread evenly.

2. Sprinkle both sides of steaks with garlic powder and coarsely ground black pepper to taste.

3. Drizzle both sides of steaks with olive oil, again using the back of a spoon to spread evenly over surfaces.

4. Allow steaks to marinate for 30 minutes.

5. Place both steaks in air fryer basket and cook at 390°F for 5 minutes.

6. Turn steaks over and cook until done:
   - Medium rare: additional 5 minutes
   - Medium: additional 7 minutes
   - Well done: additional 10 minutes

7. Remove steaks from air fryer basket and let sit 5 minutes. Salt to taste and serve.

> **NOTE:** To ensure that beefsteak is safe to eat, cook it to a minimum internal temperature of 145°F.

Calf's Liver

Yield: 4 servings | Prep Time: 15 minutes | Cooking Time: 4–5 minutes per batch | Total Time: 23–25 minutes

Before air fryers, we only ever ate beef liver smothered in onions, but frying it offered a pleasant surprise. It's every bit as good as fried chicken livers, if not better. Beef liver is also easier to handle when breading and cooking because the meat isn't so fragile.

---

1 pound sliced calf's liver

salt and pepper

2 eggs

2 tablespoons milk

½ cup whole wheat flour

1½ cups panko breadcrumbs

½ cup plain breadcrumbs

½ teaspoon salt

¼ teaspoon pepper

oil for misting or cooking spray

1. Cut liver slices crosswise into strips about ½-inch wide. Sprinkle with salt and pepper to taste.

2. Beat together egg and milk in a shallow dish.

3. Place wheat flour in a second shallow dish.

4. In a third shallow dish, mix together panko, plain breadcrumbs, ½ teaspoon salt, and ¼ teaspoon pepper.

5. Preheat air fryer to 390°F.

6. Dip liver strips in flour, egg wash, and then breadcrumbs, pressing in coating slightly to make crumbs stick.

7. Cooking half the liver at a time, place strips in air fryer basket in a single layer, close but not touching. Cook at 390°F for 4 to 5 minutes or until done to your preference.

8. Repeat step 7 to cook remaining liver.

Calzones South of the Border

Yield: 8 calzones | Prep Time: 30 minutes | Cooking Time: 7–8 minutes per batch | Total Time: 44–46 minutes

Tex-Mex filling offers a nice twist on traditional calzones. Pair these with black beans and roasted corn or, on the lighter side, fresh tomato and avocado slices.

Filling
¼ pound ground pork sausage
½ teaspoon chile powder
¼ teaspoon ground cumin
⅛ teaspoon garlic powder
⅛ teaspoon onion powder
⅛ teaspoon oregano
½ cup ricotta cheese
1 ounce sharp Cheddar cheese, shredded
2 ounces Pepper Jack cheese, shredded
1 4-ounce can chopped green chiles, drained

oil for misting or cooking spray
salsa, sour cream, or guacamole

Crust
2 cups white wheat flour, plus more for kneading
    and rolling
1 package (¼ ounce) RapidRise yeast
1 teaspoon salt
½ teaspoon chile powder
½ teaspoon ground cumin
1 cup warm water (115°F to 125°F)
2 teaspoons olive oil

1. Crumble sausage into air fryer baking pan and stir in the filling seasonings: chile powder, cumin, garlic powder, onion powder, and oregano. Cook at 390°F for 2 minutes. Stir, breaking apart, and cook for 3 to 4 minutes, until well done. Remove and set aside on paper towels to drain.

2. To make dough, combine flour, yeast, salt, chile powder, and cumin. Stir in warm water and oil until soft dough forms. Turn out onto lightly floured board and knead for 3 or 4 minutes. Let dough rest for 10 minutes.

3. Place the three cheeses in a medium bowl. Add cooked sausage and chiles and stir until well mixed.

4. Cut dough into 8 pieces.

5. Working with 4 pieces of the dough, press each into a circle about 5 inches in diameter. Top each dough circle with 2 heaping tablespoons of filling. Fold over into a half-moon shape and press edges together. Seal edges firmly to prevent leakage. Spray both sides with oil or cooking spray.

6. Place 4 calzones in air fryer basket and cook at 360°F for 5 minutes. Mist with oil or spray and cook for 2 to 3 minutes, until crust is done and nicely browned.

7. While the first batch is cooking, press out the remaining dough, fill, and shape into calzones.

8. Spray both sides with oil or cooking spray and cook for 5 minutes. If needed, mist with oil and continue cooking for 2 to 3 minutes longer. This second batch will cook a little faster than the first because your air fryer is already hot.

9. Serve plain or with salsa, sour cream, or guacamole.

Chicken Fried Steak

Yield: 4 servings | Prep Time: 10 minutes | Cooking Time: 15 minutes per batch | Total Time: 40 minutes

This is another southern favorite that you can make healthier by air frying. Serve it with steamed broccoli and quinoa if you like, but it's a whole lot better with a big pot of purple hull peas, corn on the cob, Okra (page 173), and sliced tomatoes fresh from the garden.

2 eggs

$\frac{1}{2}$ cup buttermilk

$1\frac{1}{2}$ cups flour

$\frac{3}{4}$ teaspoon salt

$\frac{1}{2}$ teaspoon pepper

1 pound beef cube steaks

salt and pepper

oil for misting or cooking spray

1. Beat together eggs and buttermilk in a shallow dish.

2. In another shallow dish, stir together the flour, $\frac{1}{2}$ teaspoon salt, and $\frac{1}{4}$ teaspoon pepper.

3. Season cube steaks with remaining salt and pepper to taste. Dip in flour, buttermilk egg wash, and then flour again.

4. Spray both sides of steaks with oil or cooking spray.

5. Cooking in 2 batches, place steaks in air fryer basket in single layer. Cook at 360°F for 10 minutes. Spray tops of steaks with oil and cook 5 minutes or until meat is well done.

6. Repeat to cook remaining steaks.

Greek Pita Pockets

Yield: 4 servings | Prep Time: 15 minutes | Cooking Time: 5–7 minutes | Total Time: 20–22 minutes

TASTER FAVORITE

For a lower-carb or gluten-free lunch, ditch the pita bread and convert this sandwich to a salad. Start with a plate of salad greens, pile on toppings, drizzle with dressing, and add the meatballs on the side.

Dressing
1 cup plain yogurt
1 tablespoon lemon juice
1 teaspoon dried dill weed, crushed
1 teaspoon ground oregano
$\frac{1}{2}$ teaspoon salt

Meatballs
$\frac{1}{2}$ pound ground lamb
1 tablespoon diced onion
1 teaspoon dried parsley
1 teaspoon dried dill weed, crushed
$\frac{1}{4}$ teaspoon oregano
$\frac{1}{4}$ teaspoon coriander
$\frac{1}{4}$ teaspoon ground cumin
$\frac{1}{4}$ teaspoon salt

4 pita halves

Suggested Toppings
red onion, slivered
seedless cucumber, thinly sliced
crumbled Feta cheese
sliced black olives
chopped fresh peppers

1. Stir dressing ingredients together and refrigerate while preparing lamb.

2. Combine all meatball ingredients in a large bowl and stir to distribute seasonings.

3. Shape meat mixture into 12 small meatballs, rounded or slightly flattened if you prefer.

4. Cook at 390°F for 5 to 7 minutes, until well done. Remove and drain on paper towels.

5. To serve, pile meatballs and your choice of toppings in pita pockets and drizzle with dressing.

TIP: Ground lamb with a high fat content can cause excessive smoking as it cooks. If this occurs, pause the air fryer and add several tablespoons of water to the air fryer drawer.

Italian Sausage & Peppers

Yield: 6 servings | Prep Time: 10 minutes | Cooking Time: 21–25 minutes | Total Time: 31–35 minutes

The key to this dish is not overcooking the vegetables. Cook the ingredients separately so everything turns out just right, well-done sausage and veggies at that perfect stage between crispy and tender.

1 6-ounce can tomato paste

²/₃ cup water

1 8-ounce can tomato sauce

1 teaspoon dried parsley flakes

¹/₂ teaspoon garlic powder

¹/₈ teaspoon oregano

¹/₂ pound mild Italian bulk sausage

1 tablespoon extra virgin olive oil

¹/₂ large onion, cut in 1-inch chunks

4 ounces fresh mushrooms, sliced

1 large green bell pepper, cut in 1-inch chunks

8 ounces spaghetti, cooked

Parmesan cheese for serving

1. In a large saucepan or skillet, stir together the tomato paste, water, tomato sauce, parsley, garlic, and oregano. Heat on stovetop over very low heat while preparing meat and vegetables.

2. Break sausage into small chunks, about ¹/₂-inch pieces. Place in air fryer baking pan.

3. Cook at 390°F for 5 minutes. Stir. Cook 5 to 7 minutes longer or until sausage is well done. Remove from pan, drain on paper towels, and add to the sauce mixture.

4. If any sausage grease remains in baking pan, pour it off or use paper towels to soak it up. (Be careful handling that hot pan!)

5. Place olive oil, onions, and mushrooms in pan and stir. Cook for 5 minutes or just until tender. Using a slotted spoon, transfer onions and mushrooms from baking pan into the sauce and sausage mixture.

6. Place bell pepper chunks in air fryer baking pan and cook for 6 to 8 minutes or until tender. When done, stir into sauce with sausage and other vegetables.

7. Serve over cooked spaghetti with plenty of Parmesan cheese.

> **TIP:** If you can find only Italian link sausage, either remove the casing and break up the sausage or cut it into ¹/₂-inch slices before cooking.

Kielbasa Chunks with Pineapple & Peppers

Yield: 2–4 servings | Prep Time: 15 minutes | Cooking Time: 10 minutes | Total Time: 25 minutes

GLUTEN FREE   KID PLEASER   SUPER EASY

This flavorful dish works equally well as a snack before dinner or as the star of the show. Serve it over rice for a main course or create an easy appetizer by spearing fruit and meat chunks onto long toothpicks. See insert B8 for recipe photo.

$3/4$ pound kielbasa sausage

1 cup bell pepper chunks (any color)

1 8-ounce can pineapple chunks in juice, drained

1 tablespoon barbeque seasoning

1 tablespoon soy sauce

cooking spray

1. Cut sausage into $1/2$-inch slices.

2. In a medium bowl, toss all ingredients together.

3. Spray air fryer basket with nonstick cooking spray.

4. Pour sausage mixture into the basket.

5. Cook at 390°F for approximately 5 minutes. Shake basket and cook an additional 5 minutes.

TIP: For appetizers, you may prefer smaller chunks of sausage, so trim your slices to about ¼ inch. We recommend McCormick Grill Mates Smokehouse Maple seasoning for this recipe.

Lamb Chops

Yield: 2–3 servings | Prep Time: 30 minutes | Cooking Time: 20 minutes | Total Time: 50 minutes

GLUTEN FREE   SUPER EASY   TASTER FAVORITE

Some meats don't need much help to taste great, including a good lamb chop. Be sure to try these with our Green Peas with Mint (page 163). See insert C1 for recipe photo.

---

2 teaspoons oil

½ teaspoon ground rosemary

½ teaspoon lemon juice

1 pound lamb chops, approximately 1-inch thick

salt and pepper

cooking spray

1. Mix the oil, rosemary, and lemon juice together and rub into all sides of the lamb chops. Season to taste with salt and pepper.

2. For best flavor, cover lamb chops and allow them to rest in the fridge for 15 to 20 minutes.

3. Spray air fryer basket with nonstick spray and place lamb chops in it.

4. Cook at 360°F for approximately 20 minutes. This will cook chops to medium. The meat will be juicy but have no remaining pink. Cook for a minute or two longer for well done chops. For rare chops, stop cooking after about 12 minutes and check for doneness.

> **TIP:** If you have a meat thermometer, these approximate cooking temperatures may be helpful:
>
> 145°F for medium rare
> 160°F for medium
> 170°F for well done
>
> The USDA recommends that lamb chops be cooked to a minimum temperature of 145°F.

Meat Loaves

Yield: 4 servings | Prep Time: 15 minutes | Cooking Time: 17–19 minutes | Total Time: 32–34 minutes

The breadcrumbs in this recipe make a huge difference. Commercial breadcrumbs will give your meatloaf a mealy consistency. Instead, use ordinary sandwich bread or something with a similar texture, such as French bread.

Sauce

¼ cup white vinegar

¼ cup brown sugar

2 tablespoons Worcestershire sauce

½ cup ketchup

Meat Loaves

1 pound very lean ground beef

⅔ cup dry bread (approx. 1 slice torn into small pieces)

1 egg

⅓ cup minced onion

1 teaspoon salt

2 tablespoons ketchup

1. In a small saucepan, combine all sauce ingredients and bring to a boil. Remove from heat and stir to ensure that brown sugar dissolves completely.

2. In a large bowl, combine the beef, bread, egg, onion, salt, and ketchup. Mix well.

3. Divide meat mixture into 4 portions and shape each into a thick, round patty. Patties will be about 3 to 3½ inches in diameter, and all four should fit easily into the air fryer basket at once.

4. Cook at 360°F for 16 to 18 minutes, until meat is well done. Baste tops of mini loaves with a small amount of sauce, and cook 1 minute.

5. Serve hot with additional sauce on the side.

TIP: If you prefer a less tangy sauce, reduce the vinegar to 2 tablespoons or omit.

Meatball Subs

Yield: 4–8 servings | Prep Time: 15 minutes | Cooking Time: 9–11 minutes | Total Time: 24–26 minutes

You can cut these big sandwiches in half to serve 8, but for the heartiest appetites count on 1 sub per person. (If you're feeding teenagers, you know what we mean!)

Marinara Sauce

1 15-ounce can diced tomatoes

1 teaspoon garlic powder

1 teaspoon dried basil

$\frac{1}{2}$ teaspoon oregano

$\frac{1}{8}$ teaspoon salt

1 tablespoon robust olive oil

Meatballs

$\frac{1}{4}$ pound ground turkey

$\frac{3}{4}$ pound very lean ground beef

1 tablespoon milk

$\frac{1}{2}$ cup torn bread pieces

1 egg

$\frac{1}{4}$ teaspoon salt

$\frac{1}{2}$ teaspoon dried onion

1 teaspoon garlic powder

$\frac{1}{4}$ teaspoon smoked paprika

$\frac{1}{4}$ teaspoon crushed red pepper

$1\frac{1}{2}$ teaspoons dried parsley

$\frac{1}{4}$ teaspoon oregano

2 teaspoons Worcestershire sauce

Sandwiches

4 large whole-grain sub or hoagie rolls, split

toppings, sliced or chopped:

mushrooms

jalapeño or banana peppers

red or green bell pepper

red onions

grated cheese

1. Place all marinara ingredients in saucepan and bring to a boil. Lower heat and simmer 10 minutes, uncovered.

2. Combine all meatball ingredients in large bowl and stir. Mixture should be well blended but don't overwork it. Excessive mixing will toughen the meatballs.

3. Divide meat into 16 equal portions and shape into balls.

4. Cook the balls at 360°F until meat is done and juices run clear, about 9 to 11 minutes.

5. While meatballs are cooking, taste marinara. If you prefer stronger flavors, add more seasoning and simmer another 5 minutes.

6. When meatballs finish cooking, drain them on paper towels.

7. To assemble subs, place 4 meatballs on each sub roll, spoon sauce over meat, and add preferred toppings. Serve with additional marinara for dipping.

> **TIP:** For best results, don't use commercial bread-crumbs for the meatballs. Instead, use any ordinary sandwich bread torn into small pieces.

Natchitoches Meat Pies

Yield: 8 pies | Prep Time: 20 minutes | Cooking Time: meat 10–12 minutes; pies 6 minutes per batch | Total Time: 42–44 minutes

Natchitoches (*NAK-a-tish*), established in 1714, is the oldest permanent settlement in the Louisiana Purchase and is famous for two things. One is the Christmas Festival of Lights, as depicted in the movie *Steel Magnolias*. The other is these spicy meat pies.

Filling
½ pound lean ground beef
¼ cup finely chopped onion
¼ cup finely chopped green bell pepper
⅛ teaspoon salt
½ teaspoon garlic powder
½ teaspoon red pepper flakes
1 tablespoon low sodium Worcestershire sauce

Crust
2 cups self-rising flour
¼ cup butter, finely diced
1 cup milk

Egg Wash
1 egg
1 tablespoon water or milk

oil for misting or cooking spray

1. Mix all filling ingredients well and shape into 4 small patties.

2. Cook patties in air fryer basket at 390°F for 10 to 12 minutes or until well done.

3. Place patties in large bowl and use fork and knife to crumble meat into very small pieces. Set aside.

4. To make the crust, use a pastry blender or fork to cut the butter into the flour until well mixed. Add milk and stir until dough stiffens.

5. Divide dough into 8 equal portions.

6. On a lightly floured surface, roll each portion of dough into a circle. The circle should be thin and about 5 inches in diameter, but don't worry about getting a perfect shape. Uneven circles result in a rustic look that many people prefer.

7. Spoon 2 tablespoons of meat filling onto each dough circle.

8. Brush egg wash all the way around the edge of dough circle, about ½-inch deep. (See Tip.)

9. Fold each circle in half and press dough with tines of a dinner fork to seal the edges all the way around.

10. Brush tops of sealed meat pies with egg wash.

11. Cook filled pies in a single layer in air fryer basket at 360°F for 4 minutes. Spray tops with oil or cooking spray, turn pies over, and spray bottoms with oil or cooking spray. Cook for an additional 2 minutes.

12. Repeat previous step to cook remaining pies.

TIP: These meat pies also freeze well. To cook frozen pies, do not thaw them. Omit the egg wash and spray both sides of frozen pies with oil. Cook at 360°F for 8 minutes. Turn pies over, spray bottoms again, and cook for an additional 2 minutes.

Pepperoni Pockets

Yield: 4 servings | Prep Time: 10 minutes | Cooking Time: 8–10 minutes | Total Time: 18–20 minutes

KID PLEASER SUPER EASY

A plain, inexpensive loaf of French or Italian bread works just fine for these toasty sandwiches. To make them a little more special, look for a nice artisan bread, preferably a ready-to-bake loaf.

4 bread slices, 1-inch thick

olive oil for misting

24 slices pepperoni (about 2 ounces)

1 ounce roasted red peppers, drained and patted dry

1 ounce Pepper Jack cheese cut into 4 slices

pizza sauce (optional)

1. Spray both sides of bread slices with olive oil.

2. Stand slices upright and cut a deep slit in the top to create a pocket—almost to the bottom crust but not all the way through.

3. Stuff each bread pocket with 6 slices of pepperoni, a large strip of roasted red pepper, and a slice of cheese.

4. Place bread pockets in air fryer basket, standing up. Cook at 360°F for 8 to 10 minutes, until filling is heated through and bread is lightly browned. Serve while hot as is or with pizza sauce for dipping.

NOTE: "Ready-to-bake" bread has been partially cooked so you bake it only long enough to heat it and brown the outside. If you use one of these, you don't need to bake it first. Use your unbaked bread as is, following the exact steps above.

Pizza Tortilla Rolls

Yield: 4 servings | Prep Time: 15 minutes | Cooking Time: 7–8 minutes per batch | Total Time: 29–31 minutes

KID PLEASER   SUPER EASY

These Italian-style taquitos are deliciously messy to eat. For a neater rollup, omit the sauce and serve it on the side for dipping.

---

1 teaspoon butter

½ medium onion, slivered

½ red or green bell pepper, julienned

4 ounces fresh white mushrooms, chopped

8 flour tortillas (6- or 7-inch size)

½ cup pizza sauce

8 thin slices deli ham

24 pepperoni slices (about 1½ ounces)

1 cup shredded mozzarella cheese (about 4 ounces)

oil for misting or cooking spray

1. Place butter, onions, bell pepper, and mushrooms in air fryer baking pan. Cook at 390°F for 3 minutes. Stir and cook 3 to 4 minutes longer until just crisp and tender. Remove pan and set aside.

2. To assemble rolls, spread about 2 teaspoons of pizza sauce on one half of each tortilla. Top with a slice of ham and 3 slices of pepperoni. Divide sautéed vegetables among tortillas and top with cheese.

3. Roll up tortillas, secure with toothpicks if needed, and spray with oil.

4. Place 4 rolls in air fryer basket and cook for 4 minutes. Turn and cook 3 to 4 minutes, until heated through and lightly browned.

5. Repeat step 4 to cook remaining pizza rolls.

> **TIP:** Don't overfill your rolls. Keep the filling an inch from the tortilla edges all around. If you do overload or place filling too close to edges, it will spill out during cooking. Your rolls will taste fine, but you'll lose some of your filling, and it can make a mess in your air fryer drawer.

Pork & Beef Egg Rolls

Yield: 8 egg rolls | Prep Time: 30 minutes | Cooking Time: 7–8 minutes per batch | Total Time: 44–46 minutes

Air frying works very well with egg roll wrappers, giving you lots of tasty crunch without excess grease. If you've never made egg rolls before, it isn't hard. On the back of the egg roll wraps package, you'll find an illustrated guide explaining how to roll them. Once you see how easy this is, you'll think of dozens of other fillings to use!

¼ pound very lean ground beef

¼ pound lean ground pork

1 tablespoon soy sauce

1 teaspoon olive oil

½ cup grated carrots

2 green onions, chopped

2 cups grated Napa cabbage

¼ cup chopped water chestnuts

¼ teaspoon salt

¼ teaspoon garlic powder

¼ teaspoon black pepper

1 egg

1 tablespoon water

8 egg roll wraps

oil for misting or cooking spray

1. In a large skillet, brown beef and pork with soy sauce. Remove cooked meat from skillet, drain, and set aside.

2. Pour off any excess grease from skillet. Add olive oil, carrots, and onions. Sauté until barely tender, about 1 minute.

3. Stir in cabbage, cover, and cook for 1 minute or just until cabbage slightly wilts. Remove from heat.

4. In a large bowl, combine the cooked meats and vegetables, water chestnuts, salt, garlic powder, and pepper. Stir well. If needed, add more salt to taste.

5. Beat together egg and water in a small bowl.

6. Fill egg roll wrappers, using about ¼ cup of filling for each wrap. Roll up and brush all over with egg wash to seal. Spray very lightly with olive oil or cooking spray.

7. Place 4 egg rolls in air fryer basket and cook at 390°F for 4 minutes. Turn over and cook 3 to 4 more minutes, until golden brown and crispy.

8. Repeat to cook remaining egg rolls.

TIP: If needed, drain filling in colander before placing in wrappers. Wet filling can prevent the wraps from crisping.

Pork Chops

Yield: 2 servings | Prep Time: 5 minutes | Cooking Time: 16–20 minutes | Total Time: 21–25 minutes

GLUTEN FREE   SUPER EASY   TASTER FAVORITE

For best results, don't skip the resting time after meat is cooked. Letting chops, steaks, and roasts sit for a few minutes before cutting ensures that the juices stay in the meat, giving you a flavorful, juicy dish. See insert C2 for recipe photo.

2 bone-in, centercut pork chops, 1-inch thick (10 ounces each)

2 teaspoons Worcestershire sauce

salt and pepper

cooking spray

1. Rub the Worcestershire sauce into both sides of pork chops.

2. Season with salt and pepper to taste.

3. Spray air fryer basket with cooking spray and place the chops in basket side by side.

4. Cook at 360°F for 16 to 20 minutes or until well done. Let rest for 5 minutes before serving.

Pork Cutlets with Aloha Salsa

Yield: 4 servings | Prep Time: 20 minutes | Cooking Time: 7–9 minutes | Total Time: 27–29 minutes

TASTER FAVORITE

These lightly seasoned cutlets taste delicious on their own, but the island-style salsa adds a refreshing accent. Serve with brown rice and broccoli or crisp, tender green beans.

Aloha Salsa

1 cup fresh pineapple, chopped in small pieces

¼ cup red onion, finely chopped

¼ cup green or red bell pepper, chopped

½ teaspoon ground cinnamon

1 teaspoon low-sodium soy sauce

⅛ teaspoon crushed red pepper

⅛ teaspoon ground black pepper

2 eggs

2 tablespoons milk

¼ cup flour

¼ cup panko breadcrumbs

4 teaspoons sesame seeds

1 pound boneless, thin pork cutlets (⅜- to ½-inch thick)

lemon pepper and salt

¼ cup cornstarch

oil for misting or cooking spray

1. In a medium bowl, stir together all ingredients for salsa. Cover and refrigerate while cooking pork.

2. Preheat air fryer to 390°F.

3. Beat together eggs and milk in shallow dish.

4. In another shallow dish, mix together the flour, panko, and sesame seeds.

5. Sprinkle pork cutlets with lemon pepper and salt to taste. Most lemon pepper seasoning contains salt, so go easy adding extra.

6. Dip pork cutlets in cornstarch, egg mixture, and then panko coating. Spray both sides with oil or cooking spray.

7. Cook cutlets for 3 minutes. Turn cutlets over, spraying both sides, and continue cooking for 4 to 6 minutes or until well done.

8. Serve fried cutlets with salsa on the side.

Pork Loin

Yield: 8 servings | Prep Time: 10 minutes | Cooking Time: 45–50 minutes | Total Time: 55–60 minutes

GLUTEN FREE   SUPER EASY

Leftover slices of pork roast make a delicious sandwich, especially when dressed with spicy mustard. You can tuck warmed pork slices into a hot biscuit for a change of pace at breakfast time or use your leftovers in our Cuban Sliders (page 38). See insert C1 for recipe photo.

1 tablespoon lime juice

1 tablespoon orange marmalade

1 teaspoon coarse brown mustard

1 teaspoon curry powder

1 teaspoon dried lemongrass

2-pound boneless pork loin roast

salt and pepper

cooking spray

1. Mix together the lime juice, marmalade, mustard, curry powder, and lemongrass.

2. Rub mixture all over the surface of the pork loin. Season to taste with salt and pepper.

3. Spray air fryer basket with nonstick spray and place pork roast diagonally in basket.

4. Cook at 360°F for approximately 45 to 50 minutes, until roast registers 130°F on a meat thermometer.

5. Wrap roast in foil and let rest for 10 minutes before slicing.

Sausage-Cheese Calzone

Yield: 8 calzones | Prep Time: 30 minutes | Cooking Time: 7–8 minutes per batch | Total Time: 44–46 minutes

White wheat flour is a healthier choice that makes for slightly firmer dough, which works best in an air fryer basket. The RapidRise yeast in this recipe eliminates the need for a lengthy rising time.

Crust

2 cups white wheat flour, plus more for kneading and rolling

1 package (¼ ounce) RapidRise yeast

1 teaspoon salt

½ teaspoon dried basil

1 cup warm water (115°F to 125°F)

2 teaspoons olive oil

Filling

¼ pound Italian sausage

½ cup ricotta cheese

4 ounces mozzarella cheese, shredded

¼ cup grated Parmesan cheese

oil for misting or cooking spray

marinara sauce for serving

1. Crumble Italian sausage into air fryer baking pan and cook at 390°F for 5 minutes. Stir, breaking apart, and cook for 3 to 4 minutes, until well done. Remove and set aside on paper towels to drain.

2. To make dough, combine flour, yeast, salt, and basil. Add warm water and oil and stir until a soft dough forms. Turn out onto lightly floured board and knead for 3 or 4 minutes. Let dough rest for 10 minutes.

3. To make filling, combine the three cheeses in a medium bowl and mix well. Stir in the cooked sausage.

4. Cut dough into 8 pieces.

5. Working with 4 pieces of the dough, press each into a circle about 5 inches in diameter. Top each dough circle with 2 heaping tablespoons of filling. Fold over to create a half-moon shape and press edges firmly together. Be sure that edges are firmly sealed to prevent leakage. Spray both sides with oil or cooking spray.

6. Place 4 calzones in air fryer basket and cook at 360°F for 5 minutes. Mist with oil and cook for 2 to 3 minutes, until crust is done and nicely browned.

7. While the first batch is cooking, press out the remaining dough, fill, and shape into calzones.

8. Spray both sides with oil and cook for 5 minutes. If needed, mist with oil and continue cooking for 2 to 3 minutes longer. This second batch will cook a little faster than the first because your air fryer is already hot.

9. Serve with marinara sauce on the side for dipping.

Sloppy Joes

Yield: 4 large sandwiches or 8 sliders | Prep Time: 10 minutes |
Cooking Time: meat 10–14 minutes, sloppy joe 7 minutes | Total Time: 27–31 minutes

KID PLEASER

As the name implies, these sandwiches should be sloppy to eat. If your cooked meat sauce seems a bit dry, stir in more water a tablespoon at a time until you have a nice, juicy consistency. Serve with plenty of napkins!

oil for misting or cooking spray

1 pound very lean ground beef

1 teaspoon onion powder

⅓ cup ketchup

¼ cup water

½ teaspoon celery seed

1 tablespoon lemon juice

1½ teaspoons brown sugar

1¼ teaspoons low-sodium Worcestershire sauce

½ teaspoon salt (optional)

½ teaspoon vinegar

⅛ teaspoon dry mustard

hamburger or slider buns

1. Spray air fryer basket with nonstick cooking spray or olive oil.

2. Break raw ground beef into small chunks and pile into basket.

3. Cook at 390°F for 5 minutes. Stir to break apart and cook 3 minutes. Stir and cook 2 to 4 minutes longer or until meat is well done.

4. Remove meat from air fryer, drain, and use a knife and fork to crumble into small pieces.

5. Give your air fryer basket a quick rinse to remove any bits of meat.

6. Place all the remaining ingredients except the buns in a 6 x 6-inch baking pan and mix together.

7. Add meat and stir well.

8. Cook at 330°F for 5 minutes. Stir and cook for 2 minutes.

9. Scoop onto buns.

Steak Fingers

Yield: 4 servings | Prep Time: 5 minutes | Cooking Time: 8–12 minutes per batch | Total Time: 21–29 minutes

KID PLEASER   SUPER EASY   TASTER FAVORITE

If you like chicken fried steak, this healthier version gives you great taste without all the grease and heavy batter. These steak fingers don't need a fancy dipping sauce. Serve as is or with ketchup!

4 small beef cube steaks
salt and pepper
½ cup flour
oil for misting or cooking spray

1. Cut cube steaks into 1-inch-wide strips.

2. Sprinkle lightly with salt and pepper to taste.

3. Roll in flour to coat all sides.

4. Spray air fryer basket with cooking spray or oil.

5. Place steak strips in air fryer basket in single layer, very close together but not touching. Spray top of steak strips with oil or cooking spray.

6. Cook at 390°F for 4 minutes, turn strips over, and spray with oil or cooking spray.

7. Cook 4 more minutes and test with fork for doneness. Steak fingers should be crispy outside with no red juices inside. If needed, cook an additional 2 to 4 minutes or until well done. (Don't eat beef cube steak rare.)

8. Repeat steps 5 through 7 to cook remaining strips.

Stuffed Bell Peppers

Yield: 4 servings | Prep Time: 20 minutes | Cooking Time: meat 10–12 minutes, peppers 10–12 minutes | Total Time: 40–44 minutes

We buy only one brand of canned tomatoes, Red Gold, because they're all-natural and non-GMO; they contain no MSG, artificial colors, flavors, or preservatives; and the cans feature non-BPA liners. They're also delicious! You can't beat homegrown in season, but Red Gold tastes better than any other canned brand and better than any fresh commercial tomato. If you've sworn off canned tomatoes forever, substitute 1¾ cups of crushed fresh tomatoes in the sauce.

¼ pound lean ground pork

¾ pound lean ground beef

¼ cup onion, minced

1 15-ounce can Red Gold crushed tomatoes

1 teaspoon Worcestershire sauce

1 teaspoon barbeque seasoning

1 teaspoon honey

½ teaspoon dried basil

½ cup cooked brown rice

½ teaspoon garlic powder

½ teaspoon oregano

½ teaspoon salt

2 small bell peppers

1. Place pork, beef, and onion in air fryer baking pan and cook at 360°F for 5 minutes.

2. Stir to break apart chunks and cook 3 more minutes. Continue cooking and stirring in 2-minute intervals until meat is well done. Remove from pan and drain.

3. In a small saucepan, combine the tomatoes, Worcestershire, barbeque seasoning, honey, and basil. Stir well to mix in honey and seasonings.

4. In a large bowl, combine the cooked meat mixture, rice, garlic powder, oregano, and salt. Add ¼ cup of the seasoned crushed tomatoes. Stir until well mixed.

5. Cut peppers in half and remove stems and seeds.

6. Stuff each pepper half with one fourth of the meat mixture.

7. Place the peppers in air fryer basket and cook for 10 to 12 minutes, until peppers are crisp tender.

8. Heat remaining tomato sauce. Serve peppers with warm sauce spooned over top.

> **TIP:** We recommend McCormick Grill Mates Smokehouse Maple seasoning for this recipe.

Venison Backstrap

Yield: 4 servings | Prep Time: 10 minutes | Cooking Time: 10–12 minutes per batch | Total Time: 30–34 minutes

Backstrap is the prime cut, but this recipe works equally well with any tender deer steak. The whole wheat flour gives the coating a slightly different texture that's especially nice with venison and other game.

---

2 eggs

¼ cup milk

1 cup whole wheat flour

½ teaspoon salt

¼ teaspoon pepper

1 pound venison backstrap, sliced

salt and pepper

oil for misting or cooking spray

1. Beat together eggs and milk in a shallow dish.

2. In another shallow dish, combine the flour, salt, and pepper. Stir to mix well.

3. Sprinkle venison steaks with additional salt and pepper to taste. Dip in flour, egg wash, then in flour again, pressing in coating.

4. Spray steaks with oil or cooking spray on both sides.

5. Cooking in 2 batches, place steaks in the air fryer basket in a single layer. Cook at 360°F for 8 minutes. Spray with oil, turn over, and spray other side. Cook for 2 to 4 minutes longer, until coating is crispy brown and meat is done to your liking.

6. Repeat to cook remaining venison.

Wiener Schnitzel

Yield: 4 servings | Prep Time: 15 minutes | Cooking Time: 14–16 minutes | Total Time: 29–31 minutes

An Old World tradition, schnitzel is pounded, breaded meat, and there are about as many ways to cook it as there are regions in Europe. Some recipes insist on beef or veal, but ours uses thinly cut pork to eliminate the need for vigorous pounding.

4 thin boneless pork loin chops

2 tablespoons lemon juice

½ cup flour

1 teaspoon salt

¼ teaspoon marjoram

1 cup plain breadcrumbs

2 eggs, beaten

oil for misting or cooking spray

1. Rub the lemon juice into all sides of pork chops.

2. Mix together the flour, salt, and marjoram.

3. Place flour mixture on a sheet of wax paper.

4. Place breadcrumbs on another sheet of wax paper.

5. Roll pork chops in flour, dip in beaten eggs, then roll in breadcrumbs. Mist all sides with oil or cooking spray.

6. Spray air fryer basket with nonstick cooking spray and place pork chops in basket.

7. Cook at 390°F for 7 minutes. Turn, mist again, and cook for another 7 or 8 minutes, until well done. Serve with lemon wedges.

FISH & SEAFOOD

Almond-Crusted Fish

Yield: 4 servings | Prep Time: 15 minutes | Cooking Time: 10 minutes | Total Time: 25 minutes

This simplified version of fish amandine cooks up fast and doesn't leave a huge mess in the kitchen. Keep it healthy by choosing a good-quality fish.

---

4 4-ounce fish fillets

¾ cup breadcrumbs

¼ cup sliced almonds, crushed

2 tablespoons lemon juice

⅛ teaspoon cayenne

salt and pepper

¾ cup flour

1 egg, beaten with 1 tablespoon water

oil for misting or cooking spray

1. Split fish fillets lengthwise down the center to create 8 pieces.

2. Mix breadcrumbs and almonds together and set aside.

3. Mix the lemon juice and cayenne together. Brush on all sides of fish.

4. Season fish to taste with salt and pepper.

5. Place the flour on a sheet of wax paper.

6. Roll fillets in flour, dip in egg wash, and roll in the crumb mixture.

7. Mist both sides of fish with oil or cooking spray.

8. Spray air fryer basket and lay fillets inside.

9. Cook at 390°F for 5 minutes, turn fish over, and cook for an additional 5 minutes or until fish is done and flakes easily.

Fried Pickles, page 44

Roasted Chickpeas, page 56

Eggplant Fries, page 39

Buttermilk-Fried Drumsticks, page 68

Chicken Nuggets, page 73

String Bean Fries, page 60

Boneless Ribeyes, page 92

Cornish Hens with Honey-Lime Glaze, page 79

Turkey Burgers, page 89

Kielbasa Chunks with Pineapple and Peppers, page 98

Onion Rings, page 174

Blackened Red Snapper

Yield: 4 servings | Prep Time: 13 minutes | Cooking Time: 8–10 minutes | Total Time: 21–23 minutes

GLUTEN FREE   SUPER EASY

Cooking blackened fish properly creates so much smoke that it's best done outdoors. But why bother with that when your air fryer can give you great taste without all the smoke? A heavy dose of black pepper gives the fish that nice blackened color. It also makes it quite spicy, but you can use less pepper if you prefer a milder taste. Topping the fish with lemon before cooking adds a subtle citrus note.

1½ teaspoons black pepper

¼ teaspoon thyme

¼ teaspoon garlic powder

⅛ teaspoon cayenne pepper

1 teaspoon olive oil

4 4-ounce red snapper fillet portions, skin on

4 thin slices lemon

cooking spray

1. Mix the spices and oil together to make a paste. Rub into both sides of the fish.

2. Spray air fryer basket with nonstick cooking spray and lay snapper steaks in basket, skin-side down.

3. Place a lemon slice on each piece of fish.

4. Cook at 390°F for 8 to 10 minutes. The fish will not flake when done, but it should be white through the center.

Catfish Nuggets

Yield: 4 servings | Prep Time: 10 minutes | Cooking Time: 7–8 minutes per batch | Total Time: 24–26 minutes

TASTER FAVORITE

Around the edges of catfish, you sometimes will find a grayish layer of fat, which gives it a fishy "off" taste. Removing that fat layer takes only a minute and results in a clean, fresh fish flavor. These nuggets are good with tartar sauce or cocktail sauce, but we've seen people dip them in everything from ranch dressing to spicy brown mustard. See insert C3 for recipe photo.

---

2 medium catfish fillets, cut in chunks (approximately 1 x 2 inch)

salt and pepper

2 eggs

2 tablespoons skim milk

½ cup cornstarch

1 cup panko breadcrumbs, crushed

oil for misting or cooking spray

1. Season catfish chunks with salt and pepper to your liking.

2. Beat together eggs and milk in a small bowl.

3. Place cornstarch in a second small bowl.

4. Place breadcrumbs in a third small bowl.

5. Dip catfish chunks in cornstarch, dip in egg wash, shake off excess, then roll in breadcrumbs.

6. Spray all sides of catfish chunks with oil or cooking spray.

7. Place chunks in air fryer basket in a single layer, leaving space between for air circulation.

8. Cook at 390°F for 4 minutes, turn, and cook an additional 3 to 4 minutes, until fish flakes easily and outside is crispy brown.

9. Repeat steps 7 and 8 to cook remaining catfish nuggets.

Coconut-Shrimp Po' Boys

Yield: 4 servings | Prep Time: 20 minutes | Cooking Time: 5 minutes per batch | Total Time: 30 minutes

TASTER FAVORITE

No trip to New Orleans is complete without eating a po' boy. This open-face version cuts calories and carbs by using only half the bread. Try the delicious coconut shrimp as a main course with sweet and sour sauce for dipping and a baked potato and coleslaw on the side.

½ cup cornstarch

2 eggs

2 tablespoons milk

¾ cup shredded coconut

½ cup panko breadcrumbs

1 pound (31–35 count) shrimp, peeled and deveined

Old Bay Seasoning

oil for misting or cooking spray

2 large hoagie rolls

honey mustard or light mayonnaise

1½ cups shredded lettuce

1 large tomato, thinly sliced

1. Place cornstarch in a shallow dish or plate.

2. In another shallow dish, beat together eggs and milk.

3. In a third dish mix the coconut and panko crumbs.

4. Sprinkle shrimp with Old Bay Seasoning to taste.

5. Dip shrimp in cornstarch to coat lightly, dip in egg mixture, shake off excess, and roll in coconut mixture to coat well.

6. Spray both sides of coated shrimp with oil or cooking spray.

7. Cook half the shrimp in a single layer at 390°F for 5 minutes.

8. Repeat to cook remaining shrimp.

To Assemble

1. Split each hoagie lengthwise, leaving one long edge intact.

2. Place in air fryer basket and cook at 390°F for 1 to 2 minutes or until heated through.

3. Remove buns, break apart, and place on 4 plates, cut side up.

4. Spread with honey mustard and/or mayonnaise.

5. Top with shredded lettuce, tomato slices, and coconut shrimp.

Crab Cakes on a Budget

Yield: 4 servings | Prep Time: 20 minutes | Cooking Time: 10–12 minutes | Total Time: 30–32 minutes

When you're craving seafood but have more month than money, give these a try. They don't exactly like those made with good fresh lump crabmeat, but, at a tenth of the price, sometimes imitation crab is good enough to tide you over.

8 ounces imitation crabmeat

4 ounces leftover cooked fish (such as cod, pollock, or haddock)

2 tablespoons minced green onion

2 tablespoons minced celery

¾ cup crushed saltine cracker crumbs

2 tablespoons light mayonnaise

1 teaspoon prepared yellow mustard

1 tablespoon Worcestershire sauce, plus 2 teaspoons

2 teaspoons dried parsley flakes

½ teaspoon dried dill weed, crushed

½ teaspoon garlic powder

½ teaspoon Old Bay Seasoning

½ cup panko breadcrumbs

oil for misting or cooking spray

1. Use knives or a food processor to finely shred crabmeat and fish.

2. In a large bowl, combine all ingredients except panko and oil. Stir well.

3. Shape into 8 small, fat patties. (See tip.)

4. Carefully roll patties in panko crumbs to coat. Spray both sides with oil or cooking spray.

5. Place patties in air fryer basket and cook at 390°F for 10 to 12 minutes or until golden brown and crispy.

> **TIP:** If you don't have any leftover fish, increase the amount of imitation crabmeat to 12 ounces.
>
> If crab mixture is too dry to shape into patties, add a little more mayonnaise or some beaten egg white to help bind the ingredients together.

Fish Cakes

Yield: 4 servings | Prep Time: 30 minutes | Cooking Time: 10–12 minutes | Total Time: 40–42 minutes

The preparation time above applies only when you start from scratch. If you're using leftover fish and potatoes, making these fish cakes takes even less time.

¾ cup mashed potatoes (about 1 large russet potato)

12 ounces cod or other white fish

salt and pepper

oil for misting or cooking spray

1 large egg

¼ cup potato starch

½ cup panko breadcrumbs

1 tablespoon fresh chopped chives

2 tablespoons minced onion

1. Peel potatoes, cut into cubes, and cook on stovetop till soft.

2. Salt and pepper raw fish to taste. Mist with oil or cooking spray, and cook in air fryer at 360°F for 6 to 8 minutes, until fish flakes easily. If fish is crowded, rearrange halfway through cooking to ensure all pieces cook evenly.

3. Transfer fish to a plate and break apart to cool.

4. Beat egg in a shallow dish.

5. Place potato starch in another shallow dish, and panko crumbs in a third dish.

6. When potatoes are done, drain in colander and rinse with cold water.

7. In a large bowl, mash the potatoes and stir in the chives and onion. Add salt and pepper to taste, then stir in the fish.

8. If needed, stir in a tablespoon of the beaten egg to help bind the mixture. (See tip.)

9. Shape into 8 small, fat patties. Dust lightly with potato starch, dip in egg, and roll in panko crumbs. Spray both sides with oil or cooking spray.

10. Cook at 360°F for 10 to 12 minutes, until golden brown and crispy.

> **TIP:** If your mixture is too wet to stick together, add 1 or 2 tablespoons of dry breadcrumbs, often a helpful addition when using leftover mashed potatoes.

Fish Sticks for Grown-ups

Yield: 4 servings | Prep Time: 20 minutes | Cooking Time: 6–9 minutes | Total Time: 26–29 minutes

SUPER EASY

Unlike our Fish Sticks for Kids (right), these have a spicy kick. Of course, it isn't really about age. Anyone who thinks plain fish sticks are boring will prefer this more flavorful version. See insert C6 for recipe photo.

---

1 pound fish fillets

½ teaspoon hot sauce

1 tablespoon coarse brown mustard

1 teaspoon Worcestershire sauce

salt

Crumb Coating

¾ cup panko breadcrumbs

¼ cup stone-ground cornmeal

¼ teaspoon salt

oil for misting or cooking spray

1. Cut fish fillets crosswise into slices 1-inch wide.

2. Mix the hot sauce, mustard, and Worcestershire sauce together to make a paste and rub on all sides of the fish. Season to taste with salt.

3. Mix crumb coating ingredients together and spread on a sheet of wax paper.

4. Roll the fish fillets in the crumb mixture.

5. Spray all sides with olive oil or cooking spray and place in air fryer basket in a single layer.

6. Cook at 390°F for 6 to 9 minutes, until fish flakes easily.

Fish Sticks for Kids

Yield: 8 fish sticks | Prep Time: 10 minutes | Cooking Time: 6–8 minutes | Total Time: 16–18 minutes

KID PLEASER   SUPER EASY

There's nothing fancy about these fish sticks because kids like them plain and simple. This recipe is perfect for toddlers or other young ones who would recoil at even a hint of garlic or some other delicious seasoning. This recipe gives you the taste of commercial fish sticks but without any unwanted additives.

---

8 ounces fish fillets (pollock or cod)

salt (optional)

$\frac{1}{2}$ cup plain breadcrumbs

oil for misting or cooking spray

1. Cut fish fillets into "fingers" about $\frac{1}{2}$ x 3 inches. Sprinkle with salt to taste, if desired.

2. Roll fish in breadcrumbs. Spray all sides with oil or cooking spray.

3. Place in air fryer basket in single layer and cook at 390°F for 6 to 8 minutes, until golden brown and crispy.

TIP: Your cooking time can vary slightly depending on the thickness of the fish sticks. They're done when the outside is crispy and the inside flakes easily.

Fish Tacos with Jalapeño-Lime Sauce

Yield: 4 servings | Prep Time: 25 minutes | Cooking Time: 7–10 minutes | Total Time: 32–35 minutes

Serve these with either corn or flour tortillas. The Napa Cabbage Garnish adds a nice crunch that perfectly complements the fish. See insert C7 for recipe photo.

Fish Tacos
1 pound fish fillets
$1/4$ teaspoon cumin
$1/4$ teaspoon coriander
$1/8$ teaspoon ground red pepper
1 tablespoon lime zest
$1/4$ teaspoon smoked paprika
1 teaspoon oil
cooking spray
6–8 corn or flour tortillas (6-inch size)

Jalapeño-Lime Sauce
$1/2$ cup sour cream
1 tablespoon lime juice
$1/4$ teaspoon grated lime zest
$1/2$ teaspoon minced jalapeño (flesh only)
$1/4$ teaspoon cumin

Napa Cabbage Garnish
1 cup shredded Napa cabbage
$1/4$ cup slivered red or green bell pepper
$1/4$ cup slivered onion

1. Slice the fish fillets into strips approximately $1/2$-inch thick.

2. Put the strips into a sealable plastic bag along with the cumin, coriander, red pepper, lime zest, smoked paprika, and oil. Massage seasonings into the fish until evenly distributed.

3. Spray air fryer basket with nonstick cooking spray and place seasoned fish inside.

4. Cook at 390°F for approximately 5 minutes. Shake basket to distribute fish. Cook an additional 2 to 5 minutes, until fish flakes easily.

5. While the fish is cooking, prepare the Jalapeño-Lime Sauce by mixing the sour cream, lime juice, lime zest, jalapeño, and cumin together to make a smooth sauce. Set aside.

6. Mix the cabbage, bell pepper, and onion together and set aside.

7. To warm refrigerated tortillas, wrap in damp paper towels and microwave for 30 to 60 seconds.

8. To serve, spoon some of fish into a warm tortilla. Add one or two tablespoons Napa Cabbage Garnish and drizzle with Jalapeño-Lime Sauce.

TIP: For added heat, include some of the jalapeño seeds in the sauce.

Flounder Fillets

Serve these lightly crusted fillets with tartar sauce or plain ketchup and your favorite sides.

1 egg white

1 tablespoon water

1 cup panko breadcrumbs

2 tablespoons extra-light virgin olive oil

4 4-ounce flounder fillets

salt and pepper

oil for misting or cooking spray

1. Preheat air fryer to 390°F.

2. Beat together egg white and water in shallow dish.

3. In another shallow dish, mix panko crumbs and oil until well combined and crumbly (best done by hand).

4. Season flounder fillets with salt and pepper to taste. Dip each fillet into egg mixture and then roll in panko crumbs, pressing in crumbs so that fish is nicely coated.

5. Spray air fryer basket with nonstick cooking spray and add fillets. Cook at 390°F for 3 minutes.

6. Spray fish fillets but do not turn. Cook 2 to 5 minutes longer or until golden brown and crispy. Using a spatula, carefully remove fish from basket and serve.

VARIATION: For a change of pace, cut fillets into pieces and make sandwiches. Stack fish on whole wheat hamburger buns and top with shredded lettuce, tomatoes, dill pickles, red onions, and condiments to your liking.

Italian Tuna Roast

Yield: 8 servings | Prep Time: 15 minutes | Cooking Time: 21–24 minutes | Total Time: 36–39 minutes

GLUTEN FREE   TASTER FAVORITE

Seared rare tuna has become the norm in America, but in southern Italy tuna is almost always served well done. For sides, we suggest boiled new potatoes and roasted mini peppers or green beans. For more ideas, see note below.

cooking spray

1 tablespoon Italian seasoning

⅛ teaspoon ground black pepper

1 tablespoon extra-light olive oil

1 teaspoon lemon juice

1 tuna loin (approximately 2 pounds, 3 to 4 inches thick, large enough to fill a 6 x 6-inch baking dish)

1. Spray baking dish with cooking spray and place in air fryer basket. Preheat air fryer to 390°F.

2. Mix together the Italian seasoning, pepper, oil, and lemon juice.

3. Using a dull table knife or butter knife, pierce top of tuna about every half inch: Insert knife into top of tuna roast and pierce almost all the way to the bottom.

4. Spoon oil mixture into each of the holes and use the knife to push seasonings into the tuna as deeply as possible.

5. Spread any remaining oil mixture on all outer surfaces of tuna.

6. Place tuna roast in baking dish and cook at 390°F for 20 minutes. Check temperature with a meat thermometer. Cook for an additional 1 to 4 minutes or until temperature reaches 145°F.

7. Remove basket from fryer and let tuna sit in basket for 10 minutes.

NOTE: You can serve this dish piping hot or at room temperature. Use a fork to break it apart into large chunks. If you have leftovers, try it nice and cold, straight from the fridge. For a romantic dinner in front of the fireplace, open a bottle of Chianti or Tuscan red wine and serve this rustic tuna with a wedge of Parmigiano-Reggiano cheese and a good crusty loaf of bread.

Popcorn Crawfish

Yield: 4 servings | Prep Time: 15 minutes | Cooking Time: 18–20 minutes | Total Time: 33–35 minutes

Early spring in Louisiana means backyard crawfish boils, but the season is short. Frozen tail meat is available year-round, though, and the air fryer works great when you want to enjoy a tasty crunch without all the grease.

½ cup flour, plus 2 tablespoons

½ teaspoon garlic powder

1½ teaspoons Old Bay Seasoning

½ teaspoon onion powder

½ cup beer, plus 2 tablespoons

12-ounce package frozen crawfish tail meat, thawed and drained

oil for misting or cooking spray

Coating
1½ cups panko crumbs

1 teaspoon Old Bay Seasoning

½ teaspoon ground black pepper

1. In a large bowl, mix together the flour, garlic powder, Old Bay Seasoning, and onion powder. Stir in beer to blend.

2. Add crawfish meat to batter and stir to coat.

3. Combine the coating ingredients in food processor and pulse to finely crush the crumbs. Transfer crumbs to shallow dish.

4. Preheat air fryer to 390°F.

5. Pour the crawfish and batter into a colander to drain. Stir with a spoon to drain excess batter.

6. Working with a handful of crawfish at a time, roll in crumbs and place on a cookie sheet. It's okay if some of the smaller pieces of crawfish meat stick together.

7. Spray breaded crawfish with oil or cooking spray and place all at once into air fryer basket.

8. Cook at 390°F for 5 minutes. Shake basket or stir and mist again with olive oil or spray. Cook 5 more minutes, shake basket again, and mist lightly again. Continue cooking 3 to 5 more minutes, until browned and crispy.

Salmon

Yield: 4 servings | Prep Time: 35 minutes | Cooking Time: 8–10 minutes | Total Time: 43–45 minutes

GLUTEN FREE SUPER EASY

Wild-caught salmon is one of the healthiest fish you can eat. We serve it often and always are looking for new ways to cook it. The marinade below adds a touch of tasty sweet-and-sour flavor that doesn't over-power the fish. See insert C5 for recipe photo.

Marinade

3 tablespoons low-sodium soy sauce

3 tablespoons rice vinegar

3 tablespoons ketchup

3 tablespoons olive oil

3 tablespoons brown sugar

1 teaspoon garlic powder

½ teaspoon ground ginger

4 salmon fillets (½-inch thick, 3 to 4 ounces each)

cooking spray

1. Mix all marinade ingredients until well blended.

2. Place salmon in sealable plastic bag or shallow container with lid. Pour marinade over fish and turn to coat well. Refrigerate for 30 minutes.

3. Drain marinade, and spray air fryer basket with cooking spray.

4. Place salmon in basket, skin-side down.

5. Cook at 360°F for 8 to 10 minutes, watching closely to avoid overcooking. Salmon is done when just beginning to flake and still very moist.

Salmon Croquettes

Yield: 4 servings | Prep Time: 10 minutes | Cooking Time: 7–8 minutes | Total Time: 17–18 minutes

SUPER EASY

When buying canned salmon, look for wild-caught pink, sockeye, or red varieties. Generally speaking, almost all Atlantic salmon is farmed, and almost all Alaskan salmon is wild-caught.

---

1 tablespoon oil

½ cup breadcrumbs

1 14.75-ounce can salmon, drained and all skin and fat removed

1 egg, beaten

⅓ cup coarsely crushed saltine crackers (about 8 crackers)

½ teaspoon Old Bay Seasoning

½ teaspoon onion powder

½ teaspoon Worcestershire sauce

1. Preheat air fryer to 390°F.

2. In a shallow dish, mix oil and breadcrumbs until crumbly.

3. In a large bowl, combine the salmon, egg, cracker crumbs, Old Bay, onion powder, and Worcestershire. Mix well and shape into 8 small patties about ½-inch thick.

4. Gently dip each patty into breadcrumb mixture and turn to coat well on all sides.

5. Cook at 390°F for 7 to 8 minutes or until outside is crispy and browned.

Sea Scallops

Yield: 4 servings | Prep Time: 10 minutes | Cooking Time: 6–8 minutes per batch | Total Time: 22–26 minutes

TASTER FAVORITE

Scallops are so delicate and flavorful that we like to keep it simple with both the seasoning and the coating. For a bolder taste, use Old Bay Seasoning instead of salt and pepper, and for more crunch, substitute panko for the plain breadcrumbs.

1½ pounds sea scallops

salt and pepper

2 eggs

½ cup flour

½ cup plain breadcrumbs

oil for misting or cooking spray

1. Rinse scallops and remove the tough side muscle. Sprinkle to taste with salt and pepper.

2. Beat eggs together in a shallow dish. Place flour in a second shallow dish and breadcrumbs in a third.

3. Preheat air fryer to 390°F.

4. Dip scallops in flour, then eggs, and then roll in breadcrumbs. Mist with oil or cooking spray.

5. Place scallops in air fryer basket in a single layer, leaving some space between. You should be able to cook about a dozen at a time.

6. Cook at 390°F for 6 to 8 minutes, watching carefully so as not to overcook. Scallops are done when they turn opaque all the way through. They will feel slightly firm when pressed with tines of a fork.

7. Repeat step 6 to cook remaining scallops.

Shrimp

Yield: 4 servings | Prep Time: 1 hour 20 minutes | Cooking Time: 6–8 minutes per batch | Total Time: 1 hour 32–36 minutes

SUPER EASY   TASTER FAVORITE

You're going to like these fried shrimp so much that you'll never want deep-fried again. See insert C4 for recipe photo.

---

1 pound (26–30 count) shrimp, peeled, deveined, and butterflied (last tail section of shell intact)

Marinade
1 5-ounce can evaporated milk
2 eggs, beaten
2 tablespoons white vinegar
1 tablespoon baking powder

Coating
1 cup crushed panko breadcrumbs
1/2 teaspoon paprika
1/2 teaspoon Old Bay Seasoning
1/4 teaspoon garlic powder

oil for misting or cooking spray

1. Stir together all marinade ingredients until well mixed. Add shrimp and stir to coat. Refrigerate for 1 hour.

2. When ready to cook, preheat air fryer to 390°F.

3. Combine coating ingredients in shallow dish.

4. Remove shrimp from marinade, roll in crumb mixture, and spray with olive oil or cooking spray.

5. Cooking in two batches, place shrimp in air fryer basket in single layer, close but not overlapping. Cook at 390°F for 6 to 8 minutes, until light golden brown and crispy.

6. Repeat step 5 to cook remaining shrimp.

Shrimp & Grits

Yield: 4 servings | Prep Time: 15 minutes | Cooking Time: shrimp 5–7 minutes, grits 13–14 minutes | Total Time: 33–36 minutes

GLUTEN FREE   TASTER FAVORITE

Many restaurant menus in Louisiana offer this dish, and our version is quick and easy to make at home. Enjoy this flavorful recipe when you're not in the mood to dress for dinner or to stand in line waiting for a table.

1 pound raw shelled shrimp, deveined (26–30 count or smaller)

Marinade
2 tablespoons lemon juice
2 tablespoons Worcestershire sauce
1 tablespoon olive oil
1 teaspoon Old Bay Seasoning
½ teaspoon hot sauce

Grits
¾ cup quick cooking grits (not instant)
3 cups water
½ teaspoon salt
1 tablespoon butter
½ cup chopped green bell pepper
½ cup chopped celery
½ cup chopped onion
½ teaspoon oregano
¼ teaspoon Old Bay Seasoning
2 ounces sharp Cheddar cheese, grated

1. Stir together all marinade ingredients. Pour marinade over shrimp and set aside.

2. For grits, heat water and salt to boil in saucepan on stovetop. Stir in grits, lower heat to medium-low, and cook about 5 minutes or until thick and done.

3. Place butter, bell pepper, celery, and onion in air fryer baking pan. Cook at 390°F for 2 minutes and stir. Cook 6 or 7 minutes longer, until crisp tender.

4. Add oregano and 1 teaspoon Old Bay to cooked vegetables. Stir in grits and cheese and cook at 390°F for 1 minute. Stir and cook 1 to 2 minutes longer to melt cheese.

5. Remove baking pan from air fryer. Cover with plate to keep warm while shrimp cooks.

6. Drain marinade from shrimp. Place shrimp in air fryer basket and cook at 360°F for 3 minutes. Stir or shake basket. Cook 2 to 4 more minutes, until done.

7. To serve, spoon grits onto plates and top with shrimp.

TIP: If you don't like spicy heat, use only a few drops of hot sauce or omit it altogether.

Shrimp Patties

Yield: 4 servings | Prep Time: 15 minutes | Cooking Time: 10–12 minutes per batch | Total Time: 35–39 minutes

We use sushi rice in this recipe for its stickiness. Your patties will hold together better without needing eggs or other binding ingredients.

½ pound shelled and deveined raw shrimp

¼ cup chopped red bell pepper

¼ cup chopped green onion

¼ cup chopped celery

2 cups cooked sushi rice

½ teaspoon garlic powder

½ teaspoon Old Bay Seasoning

½ teaspoon salt

2 teaspoons Worcestershire sauce

½ cup plain breadcrumbs

oil for misting or cooking spray

1. Finely chop the shrimp. You can do this in a food processor, but it takes only a few pulses. Be careful not to overprocess into mush.

2. Place shrimp in a large bowl and add all other ingredients except the breadcrumbs and oil. Stir until well combined.

3. Preheat air fryer to 390°F.

4. Shape shrimp mixture into 8 patties, no more than ½-inch thick. Roll patties in breadcrumbs and mist with oil or cooking spray.

5. Place 4 shrimp patties in air fryer basket and cook at 390°F for 10 to 12 minutes, until shrimp cooks through and outside is crispy.

6. Repeat step 5 to cook remaining shrimp patties.

> **TIP:** Shrimp count or size doesn't matter. To save money, buy small shrimp because they usually are more affordable. To save time, buy big shrimp so you'll have fewer to peel. Also, keep your patties fairly thin so they cook quickly. Prolonged cooking can make the rice too crispy—not burned but harder than pleasant.

Stuffed Shrimp

Yield: 4 servings | Prep Time: 20 minutes | Cooking Time: 12 minutes per batch | Total Time: 44 minutes

TASTER FAVORITE

With these crab-stuffed shrimp as a main dish, all you need for sides are plain baked potatoes and a simple tossed salad. That's fine dining fast—a restaurant-worthy dinner in less than an hour.

---

16 tail-on shrimp, peeled and deveined (last tail section intact)

¾ cup crushed panko breadcrumbs

oil for misting or cooking spray

Stuffing

2 6-ounce cans lump crabmeat

2 tablespoons chopped shallots

2 tablespoons chopped green onions

2 tablespoons chopped celery

2 tablespoons chopped green bell pepper

½ cup crushed saltine crackers

1 teaspoon Old Bay Seasoning

1 teaspoon garlic powder

¼ teaspoon ground thyme

2 teaspoons dried parsley flakes

2 teaspoons fresh lemon juice

2 teaspoons Worcestershire sauce

1 egg, beaten

1. Rinse shrimp. Remove tail section (shell) from 4 shrimp, discard, and chop the meat finely.

2. To prepare the remaining 12 shrimp, cut a deep slit down the back side so that the meat lies open flat. Do not cut all the way through.

3. Preheat air fryer to 360°F.

4. Place chopped shrimp in a large bowl with all of the stuffing ingredients and stir to combine.

5. Divide stuffing into 12 portions, about 2 tablespoons each.

6. Place one stuffing portion onto the back of each shrimp and form into a ball or oblong shape. Press firmly so that stuffing sticks together and adheres to shrimp.

7. Gently roll each stuffed shrimp in panko crumbs and mist with oil or cooking spray.

8. Place 6 shrimp in air fryer basket and cook at 360°F for 10 minutes. Mist with oil or spray and cook 2 minutes longer or until stuffing cooks through inside and is crispy outside.

9. Repeat step 8 to cook remaining shrimp.

Tilapia Teriyaki

Yield: 3–4 servings | Prep Time: 12 minutes | Cooking Time: 10–12 minutes | Total Time: 22–24 minutes

GLUTEN FREE   SUPER EASY

Tilapia is popular for its mild flavor and low cost, but it has earned a bad reputation. It has fewer omega-3s than many other types of fish, but it's high in protein and low in fat. Choose the origin wisely. Tilapia farms in Canada and America usually rate well. Look for certifications that the fish farm meets standards for food safety, environmental accountability, and other important factors.

4 tablespoons teriyaki sauce

1 tablespoon pineapple juice

1 pound tilapia fillets

cooking spray

6 ounces frozen mixed peppers with onions, thawed and drained

2 cups cooked rice

1. Mix the teriyaki sauce and pineapple juice together in a small bowl.

2. Split tilapia fillets down the center lengthwise.

3. Brush all sides of fish with the sauce, spray air fryer basket with nonstick cooking spray, and place fish in the basket.

4. Stir the peppers and onions into the remaining sauce and spoon over the fish. Save any leftover sauce for drizzling over the fish when serving.

5. Cook at 360°F for 10 to 12 minutes, until fish flakes easily with a fork and is done in center.

6. Divide into 3 or 4 servings and serve each with approximately ½ cup cooked rice.

Tuna Nuggets in Hoisin Sauce

Yield: 4 servings | Prep Time: 15 minutes | Cooking Time: 5–7 minutes | Total Time: 20–22 minutes

GLUTEN FREE   SUPER EASY   TASTER FAVORITE

Here in America, most of us usually eat tuna only lightly seared and still rare inside. That isn't the case in other parts of the world. Keep an open mind and you may be surprised. Our taste testers were skeptical too, yet this turned out to be one of our most popular dishes.

½ cup hoisin sauce

2 tablespoons rice wine vinegar

2 teaspoons sesame oil

1 teaspoon garlic powder

2 teaspoons dried lemongrass

¼ teaspoon red pepper flakes

½ small onion, quartered and thinly sliced

8 ounces fresh tuna, cut into 1-inch cubes

cooking spray

3 cups cooked jasmine rice

1. Mix the hoisin sauce, vinegar, sesame oil, and seasonings together.

2. Stir in the onions and tuna nuggets.

3. Spray air fryer baking pan with nonstick spray and pour in tuna mixture.

4. Cook at 390°F for 3 minutes. Stir gently.

5. Cook 2 minutes and stir again, checking for doneness. Tuna should be barely cooked through, just beginning to flake and still very moist. If necessary, continue cooking and stirring in 1-minute intervals until done.

6. Serve warm over hot jasmine rice.

VARIATION: When the price of tuna is sky high, use pork loin instead. Cut the meat into ½-inch chunks and follow directions above, except in step 4 cook for 10 minutes. Stir, then continue cooking for 4 or 5 minutes, until pork is well done.

Meatless Main Dishes

Cheese Ravioli

Yield: 4 servings | Prep Time: 10 minutes | Cooking Time: 9–11 minutes | Total Time: 19–21 minutes

KID PLEASER   SUPER EASY   VEGETARIAN

It doesn't get much easier than this. Serve these with your favorite marinara, alfredo, or pizza sauce, and you have a special treat that takes just minutes to prepare.

---

1 egg

¼ cup milk

1 cup breadcrumbs

2 teaspoons Italian seasoning

⅛ teaspoon ground rosemary

¼ teaspoon basil

¼ teaspoon parsley

9-ounce package uncooked cheese ravioli

¼ cup flour

oil for misting or cooking spray

1. Preheat air fryer to 390°F.

2. In a medium bowl, beat together egg and milk.

3. In a large plastic bag, mix together the breadcrumbs, Italian seasoning, rosemary, basil, and parsley.

4. Place all the ravioli and the flour in a bag or a bowl with a lid and shake to coat.

5. Working with a handful at a time, drop floured ravioli into egg wash. Remove ravioli, letting excess drip off, and place in bag with breadcrumbs.

6. When all ravioli are in the breadcrumbs' bag, shake well to coat all pieces.

7. Dump enough ravioli into air fryer basket to form one layer. Mist with oil or cooking spray. Dump the remaining ravioli on top of the first layer and mist with oil.

8. Cook for 5 minutes. Shake well and spray with oil. Break apart any ravioli stuck together and spray any spots you missed the first time.

9. Cook 4 to 6 minutes longer, until ravioli puff up and are crispy golden brown.

Egg Rolls

Yield: 4 egg rolls | Prep Time: 20 minutes | Cooking Time: 8 minutes | Total Time: 28 minutes

VEGETARIAN

To keep it simple, serve these veggie egg rolls with your favorite sweet-and-sour or soy sauce. For something different, try our Apricot-Ginger Sauce (page 78).

1 clove garlic, minced

1 teaspoon sesame oil

1 teaspoon olive oil

½ cup chopped celery

½ cup grated carrots

2 green onions, chopped

2 ounces mushrooms, chopped

2 cups shredded Napa cabbage

1 teaspoon low-sodium soy sauce

1 teaspoon cornstarch

salt

1 egg

1 tablespoon water

4 egg roll wraps

olive oil for misting or cooking spray

1. In a large skillet, sauté garlic in sesame and olive oils over medium heat for 1 minute.

2. Add celery, carrots, onions, and mushrooms to skillet. Cook 1 minute, stirring.

3. Stir in cabbage, cover, and cook for 1 minute or just until cabbage slightly wilts.

4. In a small bowl, mix soy sauce and cornstarch. Stir into vegetables to thicken. Remove from heat. Salt to taste if needed.

5. Beat together egg and water in a small bowl.

6. Divide filling into 4 portions and roll up in egg roll wraps. Brush all over with egg wash to seal.

7. Mist egg rolls very lightly with olive oil or cooking spray and place in air fryer basket.

8. Cook at 390°F for 4 minutes. Turn over and cook 3 to 4 more minutes, until golden brown and crispy.

Eggplant Parmesan

Yield: 4 servings | Prep Time: 20 minutes | Cooking Time: 7–8 minutes per batch | Total Time: 34–36 minutes

VEGETARIAN

Deep-fried eggplant can turn out very greasy, but happily the air fryer eliminates that problem. Not only is air-fried eggplant healthier, but it tastes much better than deep-fried. A tossed green salad is the only side you need, but we also love to eat this with a good garlic breadstick.

---

1 medium eggplant, 6–8 inches long

salt

1 large egg

1 tablespoon water

$2/3$ cup panko breadcrumbs

$1/3$ cup grated Parmesan cheese, plus more for servi..g

1 tablespoon Italian seasoning

$3/4$ teaspoon oregano

oil for misting or cooking spray

1 24-ounce jar marinara sauce

8 ounces spaghetti, cooked

pepper

1. Preheat air fryer to 390°F.

2. Leaving peel intact, cut eggplant into 8 round slices about $3/4$-inch thick. Salt to taste.

3. Beat egg and water in a shallow dish.

4. In another shallow dish, combine panko, Parmesan, Italian seasoning, and oregano.

5. Dip eggplant slices in egg wash and then crumbs, pressing lightly to coat.

6. Mist slices with oil or cooking spray.

7. Place 4 eggplant slices in air fryer basket and cook for 7 to 8 minutes, until brown and crispy.

8. While eggplant is cooking, heat marinara sauce.

9. Repeat step 7 to cook remaining eggplant slices.

10. To serve, place cooked spaghetti on plates and top with marinara and eggplant slices. At the table, pass extra Parmesan cheese and freshly ground black pepper.

Falafels

Yield: 12 falafels | Prep Time: 10 minutes | Cooking Time: 10 minutes | Total Time: 20 minutes

SUPER EASY   VEGETARIAN

When you're short on time but craving something hearty, using a mix makes a good compromise. If you prefer, use your own favorite recipe for homemade, then refer to our directions below for cooking time and temperature. Either way, you can enjoy falafels lower in fat but still brown and crispy.

1 pouch falafel mix
2–3 tablespoons plain breadcrumbs
oil for misting or cooking spray

1. Prepare falafel mix according to package directions.

2. Preheat air fryer to 390°F.

3. Place breadcrumbs in shallow dish or on wax paper.

4. Shape falafel mixture into 12 balls and flatten slightly. Roll in breadcrumbs to coat all sides and mist with oil or cooking spray.

5. Place falafels in air fryer basket in single layer and cook for 5 minutes. Shake basket, and continue cooking for 5 minutes, until they brown and are crispy.

> **NOTE:** One popular brand of falafel mix comes in a 6.3-ounce box and contains 2 pouches. Each pouch makes 12 falafels. Also, when falafels cook in an air fryer, their surfaces sometimes develop small cracks. This doesn't affect taste. Your falafels may not look perfect, but they won't fall apart.

Pinto Taquitos

Yield: 4 servings | Prep Time: 15 minutes | Cooking Time: 6–8 minutes per batch | Total Time: 27–33 minutes

GLUTEN FREE   VEGETARIAN

These are great for snacking but also can make a hearty meal. Good side dish choices include Spanish rice, shredded lettuce topped with pico de gallo, or even mixed fruits.

---

12 corn tortillas (6- to 7-inch size)

Filling

½ cup refried pinto beans

½ cup grated sharp Cheddar or Pepper Jack cheese

¼ cup corn kernels (if frozen, measure after thawing and draining)

2 tablespoons chopped green onion

2 tablespoons chopped jalapeño pepper (seeds and ribs removed before chopping)

½ teaspoon lime juice

½ teaspoon chile powder, plus extra for dusting

½ teaspoon cumin

½ teaspoon garlic powder

oil for misting or cooking spray

salsa, sour cream, or guacamole for dipping

1. Mix together all filling ingredients.

2. Warm refrigerated tortillas for easier rolling. (Wrap in damp paper towels and microwave for 30 to 60 seconds.)

3. Working with one at a time, place 1 tablespoon of filling on tortilla and roll up. Spray with oil or cooking spray and dust outside with chile powder to taste.

4. Place 6 taquitos in air fryer basket (4 on bottom layer, 2 stacked crosswise on top). Cook at 390°F for 6 to 8 minutes, until crispy and brown.

5. Repeat step 4 to cook remaining taquitos.

6. Serve plain or with salsa, sour cream, or guacamole for dipping.

Tacos

Yield: 24 mini tacos | Prep Time: 10 minutes | Cooking Time: 8–10 minutes per batch | Total Time: 26–30 minutes

GLUTEN FREE   KID PLEASER   SUPER EASY   VEGETARIAN

Tacos are supposed to be easy to eat on the go without any fussy accompaniments. When you're not on the run, they taste great dipped in guacamole or even a little good-quality, low-fat sour cream. They also make an easy, delicious lunch without all the mess from deep frying.

1 24-count package 4-inch corn tortillas

1½ cups refried beans (about ¾ of a 15-ounce can)

4 ounces sharp Cheddar cheese, grated

½ cup salsa

oil for misting or cooking spray

1. Preheat air fryer to 390°F.

2. Wrap refrigerated tortillas in damp paper towels and microwave for 30 to 60 seconds to warm. If necessary, rewarm tortillas as you go to keep them soft enough to fold without breaking.

3. Working with one tortilla at a time, top with 1 tablespoon of beans, 1 tablespoon of grated cheese, and 1 teaspoon of salsa. Fold over and press down very gently on the center. Press edges firmly all around to seal. Spray both sides with oil or cooking spray.

4. Cooking in two batches, place half the tacos in the air fryer basket. To cook 12 at a time, you may need to stand them upright and lean some against the sides of basket. It's okay if they're crowded as long as you leave a little room for air to circulate around them.

5. Cook for 8 to 10 minutes or until golden brown and crispy.

6. Repeat steps 4 and 5 to cook remaining tacos.

> **TIP:** To spice these up, add a sliver of jalapeño pepper, but don't overfill the tacos. If you do, they'll leak and fall apart while cooking.

Vegetable Couscous

Yield: 4 servings | Prep Time: 15 minutes | Cooking Time: 10–12 minutes | Total Time: 25–27 minutes

VEGETARIAN

Make this for a light summer supper that doesn't keep you stuck in a hot kitchen. Serve with fresh home-grown tomatoes or add a colorful array of cantaloupe, honeydew, and watermelon slices on the side.

4 ounces white mushrooms, sliced

½ medium green bell pepper, julienned

1 cup cubed zucchini

¼ small onion, slivered

1 stalk celery, thinly sliced

¼ teaspoon ground coriander

¼ teaspoon ground cumin

salt and pepper

1 tablespoon olive oil

Couscous

¾ cup uncooked couscous

1 cup vegetable broth or water

½ teaspoon salt (omit if using salted broth)

1. Combine all vegetables in large bowl. Sprinkle with coriander, cumin, and salt and pepper to taste. Stir well, add olive oil, and stir again to coat vegetables evenly.

2. Place vegetables in air fryer basket and cook at 390°F for 5 minutes. Stir and cook for 5 to 7 more minutes, until tender.

3. While vegetables are cooking, prepare the couscous: Place broth or water and salt in large saucepan. Heat to boiling, stir in couscous, cover, and remove from heat.

4. Let couscous sit for 5 minutes, stir in cooked vegetables, and serve hot.

VARIATION: In spring, we like to substitute fresh asparagus for half or all of the zucchini.

Vegetable Hand Pies

Yield: 8 mini pies | Prep Time: 15 minutes | Cooking Time: 10 minutes per batch | Total Time: 35 minutes

VEGETARIAN

These easy-to-eat pies don't have to be piping hot to be delicious, which makes them perfect for an impromptu picnic. Add them to a basket with some fresh fruit and a thermos of iced tea, grab a blanket, and head for a nice patch of grass. After all, food always tastes better when you eat outside!

¾ cup vegetable broth

8 ounces potatoes

¾ cup frozen chopped broccoli, thawed

¼ cup chopped mushrooms

1 tablespoon cornstarch

1 tablespoon milk

1 can organic flaky biscuits (8 large biscuits)

oil for misting or cooking spray

1. Place broth in medium saucepan over low heat.

2. While broth is heating, grate raw potato into a bowl of water to prevent browning. You will need ¾ cup grated potato.

3. Roughly chop the broccoli.

4. Drain potatoes and put them in the broth along with the broccoli and mushrooms. Cook on low for 5 minutes.

5. Dissolve cornstarch in milk, then stir the mixture into the broth. Cook about a minute, until mixture thickens a little. Remove from heat and cool slightly.

6. Separate each biscuit into 2 rounds. Divide vegetable mixture evenly over half the biscuit rounds, mounding filling in the center of each.

7. Top the four rounds with filling, then the other four rounds and crimp the edges together with a fork.

8. Spray both sides with oil or cooking spray and place 4 pies in a single layer in the air fryer basket.

9. Cook at 330°F for approximately 10 minutes.

10. Repeat with the remaining biscuits. The second batch may cook more quickly because the fryer will be hot.

> **TIP:** Flaky-style biscuits are easier to separate. For other biscuits, use a thin, serrated knife and a lateral sawing motion to cut them in half crosswise.

Veggie Burgers

Yield: 4 servings | Prep Time: 15 minutes | Cooking Time: 15 minutes | Total Time: 30 minutes

GLUTEN FREE   SUPER EASY   VEGETARIAN

Serve this healthy bean patty with a side of quinoa or brown rice and a salad of tomatoes and avocados for a Meatless Monday dinner.

---

2 cans black beans, rinsed and drained

½ cup cooked quinoa

½ cup shredded raw sweet potato

¼ cup diced red onion

2 teaspoons ground cumin

1 teaspoon coriander powder

½ teaspoon salt

oil for misting or cooking spray

8 slices bread

suggested toppings: lettuce, tomato, red onion, Pepper Jack cheese, guacamole

1. In a medium bowl, mash the beans with a fork.

2. Add the quinoa, sweet potato, onion, cumin, coriander, and salt and mix well with the fork.

3. Shape into 4 patties, each ¾-inch thick.

4. Mist both sides with oil or cooking spray and also mist the basket.

5. Cook at 390°F for 15 minutes.

6. Follow the recipe for Toast, Plain & Simple (page 225).

7. Pop the veggie burgers back in the air fryer for a minute or two to reheat if necessary.

8. Serve on the toast with your favorite burger toppings.

VEGETABLES & SIDES

Asparagus

Yield: 4 servings | Prep Time: 5 minutes | Cooking Time: 9–10 minutes | Total Time: 14–15 minutes

GLUTEN FREE   SUPER EASY   TASTER FAVORITE   VEGETARIAN

Asparagus is one of our favorite vegetables, and this is our favorite way to eat it. Simple seasonings don't overpower the natural flavor, and the air fryer does a beautiful job of roasting it to perfection.

1 bunch asparagus (approx. 1 pound), washed and trimmed

⅛ teaspoon dried tarragon, crushed

salt and pepper

1 to 2 teaspoons extra-light olive oil

1. Spread asparagus spears on cookie sheet or cutting board.

2. Sprinkle with tarragon, salt, and pepper.

3. Drizzle with 1 teaspoon of oil and roll the spears or mix by hand. If needed, add up to 1 more teaspoon of oil and mix again until all spears are lightly coated.

4. Place spears in air fryer basket. If necessary, bend the longer spears to make them fit. It doesn't matter if they don't lie flat.

5. Cook at 390°F for 5 minutes. Shake basket or stir spears with a spoon.

6. Cook for an additional 4 to 5 minutes or just until crisp-tender.

Asparagus Fries

Yield: 4 servings | Prep Time: 15 minutes | Cooking Time: 5–7 minutes per batch | Total Time: 25–29 minutes

VEGETARIAN

Fried vegetables don't have to be a guilty pleasure anymore. Air frying reduces the grease to almost zero yet still creates the delicious crunch you crave. We chose a relatively light coating for these fries so as not to overpower the wonderful natural flavor of the asparagus.

---

12 ounces fresh asparagus spears with tough ends trimmed off

2 egg whites

1/4 cup water

3/4 cup panko breadcrumbs

1/4 cup grated Parmesan cheese, plus 2 tablespoons

1/4 teaspoon salt

oil for misting or cooking spray

1. Preheat air fryer to 390°F.

2. In a shallow dish, beat egg whites and water until slightly foamy.

3. In another shallow dish, combine panko, Parmesan, and salt.

4. Dip asparagus spears in egg, then roll in crumbs. Spray with oil or cooking spray.

5. Place a layer of asparagus in air fryer basket, leaving just a little space in between each spear. Stack another layer on top, crosswise. Cook at 390°F for 5 to 7 minutes, until crispy and golden brown.

6. Repeat to cook remaining asparagus.

TIP: If you want saltier fries, increase the salt in the breadcrumb mixture to taste.

Beets

Yield: 4–8 servings | Prep Time: 5 minutes | Cooking Time: 30–40 minutes | Total Time: 35–45 minutes

GLUTEN FREE   SUPER EASY   VEGETARIAN

The absolute best way to cook beets is to roast them whole. It results in the most delicious flavor and brings out all the natural sweetness. Here's how.

---

3 large beets (about 2 pounds)

1. Cut off leaves, leaving an inch of stems intact. Do not trim the root tails.

2. Wash beets and pat dry.

3. Place in air fryer basket and cook at 390°F for 30 to 40 minutes.

4. When cool enough to handle, cut off root and stem ends, peel, and slice.

> **TIP:** The cooking time above applies to 3 large beets that weigh a total of 2 pounds. This makes a *lot* of beets for salads, side dishes, soups, and other uses. If your beets aren't quite this large, they'll cook faster, so start checking them for doneness at about 20 minutes.

Broccoli Tots

Yield: 24 tots | Prep Time: 15 minutes | Cooking Time: 10 minutes | Total Time: 25 minutes

VEGETARIAN

The health benefits of broccoli are well documented, and these tots are quick and easy to make. They're also crunchy and flavorful, a delicious way to eat something good for you.

2 cups broccoli florets (about ½ pound broccoli crowns)

1 egg, beaten

⅛ teaspoon onion powder

¼ teaspoon salt

⅛ teaspoon pepper

2 tablespoons grated Parmesan cheese

¼ cup panko breadcrumbs

oil for misting

1. Steam broccoli for 2 minutes. Rinse in cold water, drain well, and chop finely.

2. In a large bowl, mix broccoli with all other ingredients except the oil.

3. Scoop out small portions of mixture and shape into 24 tots. Lay them on a cookie sheet or wax paper as you work.

4. Spray tots with oil and place in air fryer basket in single layer.

5. Cook at 390°F for 5 minutes. Shake basket and spray with oil again. Cook 5 minutes longer or until browned and crispy.

Brussels Sprouts

Yield: 3 servings | Prep Time: 5 minutes | Cooking Time: 5 minutes | Total Time: 10 minutes

GLUTEN FREE   SUPER EASY   VEGETARIAN

Fresh sprouts are delicious, but cooking them in your air fryer will fill your home with a strong aroma. We use frozen brussels sprouts instead because they cook very fast and are less pungent.

1 10-ounce package frozen brussels sprouts, thawed and halved

2 teaspoons olive oil

salt and pepper

1. Toss the brussels sprouts and olive oil together.

2. Place them in the air fryer basket and season to taste with salt and pepper.

3. Cook at 360°F for approximately 5 minutes, until the edges begin to brown.

Cauliflower

Yield: 4 servings | Prep Time: 5 minutes | Cooking Time: 5–6 minutes | Total Time: 10–11 minutes

GLUTEN FREE   SUPER EASY   VEGETARIAN

Using frozen cauliflower shortens the cooking time and leaves less of that cauliflower smell in your kitchen than when using fresh. We like it seasoned with little more than salt and pepper, but for a burst of flavor add a bit of lemon pepper seasoning or another of your favorite herbs or spices.

½ cup water

1 10-ounce package frozen cauliflower (florets)

1 teaspoon lemon pepper seasoning

1. Pour the water into air fryer drawer.

2. Pour the frozen cauliflower into the air fryer basket and sprinkle with lemon pepper seasoning.

3. Cook at 390°F for approximately 5 minutes.

> **TIP:** Cooking the cauliflower for longer than 5 minutes will brown the edges. If you prefer yours with roasted edges, cook 3 or 4 minutes longer.
>
> **VARIATION:** There are plenty of tasty ways to enjoy this dish without adding the carbs and calories of melted cheese. Try chilling your steamed cauliflower and combining it with other cooked vegetables for a filling but not fattening salad. You can make casseroles lighter by substituting steamed cauliflower for the pasta or rice.

Cheesy Potato Pot

Yield: 4 servings | Prep Time: 10 minutes | Cooking Time: 13–15 minutes | Total Time: 23–25 minutes

GLUTEN FREE   KID PLEASER   VEGETARIAN

Don't expect a velvety smooth sauce with this recipe. Enjoy the rustic feel of lightly sauced potatoes with bits of stringy cheese throughout instead. The mildly flavored sauce contrasts beautifully with nice little chunks of melted cheese to bite.

---

3 cups cubed red potatoes (unpeeled, cut into ½-inch cubes)

½ teaspoon garlic powder

salt and pepper

1 tablespoon oil

chopped chives for garnish (optional)

Sauce

2 tablespoons milk

1 tablespoon butter

2 ounces sharp Cheddar cheese, grated

1 tablespoon sour cream

1. Place potato cubes in large bowl and sprinkle with garlic, salt, and pepper. Add oil and stir to coat well.

2. Cook at 390°F for 13 to 15 minutes or until potatoes are tender. Stir every 4 or 5 minutes during cooking time.

3. While potatoes are cooking, combine milk and butter in a small saucepan. Warm over medium-low heat to melt butter. Add cheese and stir until it melts. The melted cheese will remain separated from the milk mixture. Remove from heat until potatoes are done.

4. When ready to serve, add sour cream to cheese mixture and stir over medium-low heat just until warmed. Place cooked potatoes in serving bowl. Pour sauce over potatoes and stir to combine.

5. Garnish with chives if desired.

Corn Croquettes

Yield: 4 servings | Prep Time: 10 minutes | Cooking Time: 12–14 minutes | Total Time: 22–24 minutes

TASTER FAVORITE   VEGETARIAN

You can make your croquettes any shape you like, but we prefer plain, round balls because that shape speeds up the coating and cooking processes. Place your panko crumbs in a round layer cake pan and add several corn balls at once. Move the pan in a quick circular motion, and the balls will roll around and coat themselves.

½ cup leftover mashed potatoes

2 cups corn kernels (if frozen, thawed, and well drained)

¼ teaspoon onion powder

⅛ teaspoon ground black pepper

¼ teaspoon salt

½ cup panko breadcrumbs

oil for misting or cooking spray

1. Place the potatoes and half the corn in food processor and pulse until corn is well chopped.

2. Transfer mixture to large bowl and stir in remaining corn, onion powder, pepper and salt.

3. Shape mixture into 16 balls.

4. Roll balls in panko crumbs, mist with oil or cooking spray, and place in air fryer basket.

5. Cook at 360°F for 12 to 14 minutes, until golden brown and crispy.

Corn on the Cob

Yield: 4 servings | Prep Time: 5 minutes | Cooking Time: 12–15 minutes | Total Time: 17–20 minutes

GLUTEN FREE   KID PLEASER   SUPER EASY   TASTER FAVORITE   VEGETARIAN

If you think corn is boring, you have to try it roasted. The salt is optional because whether you need it depends on the corn. In summer, when you can get locally grown corn fresh from the field, the sweet flavor is so delicious that it needs no enhancement!

---

2 large ears fresh corn

olive oil for misting

salt (optional)

1. Shuck corn, remove silks, and wash.

2. Cut or break each ear in half crosswise.

3. Spray corn with olive oil.

4. Cook at 390°F for 12 to 15 minutes or until browned as much as you like.

5. Serve plain or with coarsely ground salt.

Creole Potato Wedges

Yield: 3–4 servings | Prep Time: 5 minutes | Cooking Time: 10–15 minutes | Total Time: 15–20 minutes

SUPER EASY   TASTER FAVORITE   VEGETARIAN

These potato wedges are spicy, but they won't set your tongue on fire. If you love heat, add as much cayenne as you can handle.

---

1 pound medium Yukon gold potatoes

$\frac{1}{2}$ teaspoon cayenne pepper

$\frac{1}{2}$ teaspoon thyme

$\frac{1}{2}$ teaspoon garlic powder

$\frac{1}{2}$ teaspoon salt

$\frac{1}{2}$ teaspoon smoked paprika

1 cup dry breadcrumbs

oil for misting or cooking spray

1. Wash potatoes, cut into thick wedges, and drop wedges into a bowl of water to prevent browning.

2. Mix together the cayenne pepper, thyme, garlic powder, salt, paprika, and breadcrumbs and spread on a sheet of wax paper.

3. Remove potatoes from water and, without drying them, roll in the breadcrumb mixture.

4. Spray air fryer basket with oil or cooking spray and pile potato wedges into basket. It's okay if they form more than a single layer.

5. Cook at 390°F for 8 minutes. Shake basket, then continue cooking for 2 to 7 minutes longer, until coating is crisp and potato centers are soft. Total cooking time will vary, depending on thickness of potato wedges.

Curried Fruit

Yield: 6–8 servings | Prep Time: 10 minutes | Cooking Time: 20 minutes | Total Time: 30 minutes

GLUTEN FREE   KID PLEASER   SUPER EASY   TASTER FAVORITE   VEGETARIAN

This warm winter fruit makes a great side dish for pork and other meats, but it's equally delicious for breakfast or brunch. You might even like it as a light dessert.

---

1 cup cubed fresh pineapple

1 cup cubed fresh pear (firm, not overly ripe)

8 ounces frozen peaches, thawed

1 15-ounce can dark, sweet, pitted cherries with juice

2 tablespoons brown sugar

1 teaspoon curry powder

1. Combine all ingredients in large bowl. Stir gently to mix in the sugar and curry.

2. Pour into air fryer baking pan and cook at 360°F for 10 minutes.

3. Stir fruit and cook 10 more minutes.

4. Serve hot.

TIP: Curry is a blend of spices, so the taste can vary, depending on the blend. For this recipe, we highly recommend the McCormick brand available in most supermarkets.

Fingerling Potatoes

Yield: 4 servings | Prep Time: 5 minutes | Cooking Time: 15–20 minutes | Total Time: 20–25 minutes

GLUTEN FREE   SUPER EASY   VEGETARIAN

These are a perfect accompaniment for roasted chicken, steak, or other meats. We also like to serve them alongside a sandwich to turn a light lunch into a more substantial meal. If somehow you wind up with leftovers, serve them with breakfast instead of the usual hash browns.

1 pound fingerling potatoes
1 tablespoon light olive oil
½ teaspoon dried parsley
½ teaspoon lemon juice
coarsely ground sea salt

1. Cut potatoes in half lengthwise.

2. In a large bowl, combine potatoes, oil, parsley, and lemon juice. Stir well to coat potatoes.

3. Place potatoes in air fryer basket and cook at 360°F for 15 to 20 minutes or until lightly browned and tender inside.

4. Sprinkle with sea salt before serving.

Five-Spice Roasted Sweet Potatoes

Yield: 4 servings | Prep Time: 10 minutes | Cooking Time: 12 minutes | Total Time: 22 minutes

GLUTEN FREE   SUPER EASY   TASTER FAVORITE   VEGETARIAN

Sweet potatoes are a less starchy alternative to white spuds and provide lots of healthy nutrients and fiber. That may sound boring, but the seasoning in this recipe makes them a real taste bud treat. Plus, medical studies have shown that cinnamon and turmeric have anti-inflammatory properties.

½ teaspoon ground cinnamon

¼ teaspoon ground cumin

¼ teaspoon paprika

1 teaspoon chile powder

⅛ teaspoon turmeric

½ teaspoon salt (optional)

freshly ground black pepper

2 large sweet potatoes, peeled and cut into ¾-inch cubes (about 3 cups)

1 tablespoon olive oil

1. In a large bowl, mix together cinnamon, cumin, paprika, chile powder, turmeric, salt, and pepper to taste.

2. Add potatoes and stir well.

3. Drizzle the seasoned potatoes with the olive oil and stir until evenly coated.

4. Place seasoned potatoes in the air fryer baking pan or an ovenproof dish that fits inside your air fryer basket.

5. Cook for 6 minutes at 390°F, stop, and stir well.

6. Cook for an additional 6 minutes.

TIP: Don't overcook these! We Southerners tend to cook vegetables to mush, but that's not what you want here. These potatoes are best when cooked through but still firm. During the second cooking time, pause after 4 minutes and fork-test for doneness.

French Fries

Yield: 4 servings | Prep Time: 15 minutes | Cooking Time: 25 minutes | Total Time: 40 minutes

GLUTEN FREE   KID PLEASER   SUPER EASY   TASTER FAVORITE   VEGETARIAN

After trying these, you will never buy frozen fries again. Potatoes are one of the "Dirty Dozen" foods (highest pesticide residue), so always buy organic. For the healthiest dish, leave the peel intact for its fiber and added nutrients—not to mention its great taste! See insert C8 for recipe photo.

---

2 cups fresh potatoes

2 teaspoons oil

½ teaspoon salt

1. Cut potatoes into ½-inch-wide slices, then lay slices flat and cut into ½-inch sticks.

2. Rinse potato sticks and blot dry with a clean towel.

3. In a bowl or sealable plastic bag, mix the potatoes, oil, and salt together.

4. Pour into air fryer basket.

5. Cook at 390°F for 10 minutes. Shake basket to redistribute fries and continue cooking for approximately 15 minutes, until fries are golden brown.

Glazed Carrots

Yield: 4 servings | Prep Time: 10 minutes | Cooking Time: 8–10 minutes | Total Time: 18–20 minutes

GLUTEN FREE   KID PLEASER   SUPER EASY   VEGETARIAN

Try these carrots instead of sweet potatoes at your next Thanksgiving dinner. They complement turkey, stuffing, or dressing as well as any traditional side.

2 teaspoons honey

1 teaspoon orange juice

½ teaspoon grated orange rind

⅛ teaspoon ginger

1 pound baby carrots

2 teaspoons olive oil

¼ teaspoon salt

1. Combine honey, orange juice, grated rind, and ginger in a small bowl and set aside.

2. Toss the carrots, oil, and salt together to coat well and pour them into the air fryer basket.

3. Cook at 390°F for 5 minutes. Shake basket to stir a little and cook for 2 to 4 minutes more, until carrots are barely tender.

4. Pour carrots into air fryer baking pan.

5. Stir the honey mixture to combine well, pour glaze over carrots, and stir to coat.

6. Cook at 360°F for 1 minute or just until heated through.

Green Beans

Yield: 4 servings | Prep Time: 5 minutes | Cooking Time: 12–14 minutes | Total Time: 17–19 minutes

GLUTEN FREE   SUPER EASY   VEGETARIAN

Sometimes less is more, and simplest is best. Be careful not to overdo the salt. Depending on the sodium content of the dressing, you may not need any more salt after cooking.

---

1 pound fresh green beans

2 tablespoons Italian salad dressing

salt and pepper

1. Wash beans and snap off stem ends.

2. In a large bowl, toss beans with Italian dressing.

3. Cook at 330°F for 5 minutes. Shake basket or stir and cook 5 minutes longer. Shake basket again and, if needed, continue cooking for 2 to 4 minutes, until as tender as you like. Beans should shrivel slightly and brown in places.

4. Sprinkle with salt and pepper to taste.

> **VARIATION:** Substitute olive oil for the salad dressing and serve the cooked beans with a splash of lemon juice and balsamic vinegar—or perfectly plain.

Green Peas with Mint

Yield: 4 servings | Prep Time: 5 minutes | Cooking Time: 5 minutes | Total Time: 10 minutes

GLUTEN FREE   SUPER EASY   VEGETARIAN

This is one of our favorite side dishes with Lamb Chops (page 99). These peas also pair well with pork or chicken, and their brilliant green color adds appetizing color to any plate.

---

1 cup shredded lettuce

1 10-ounce package frozen green peas, thawed

1 tablespoon fresh mint, shredded

1 teaspoon melted butter

1. Lay the shredded lettuce in the air fryer basket.

2. Toss together the peas, mint, and melted butter and spoon over the lettuce.

3. Cook at 360°F for 5 minutes, until peas are warm and lettuce wilts.

Grits Again

Yield: varies | Prep Time: 5 minutes | Cooking Time: 10–12 minutes | Total Time: 15–17 minutes

SUPER EASY   VEGETARIAN

This recipe for using leftover grits is a very old southern tradition. If you don't have leftovers, cook your grits the day before or at least several hours early so they have plenty of time to chill.

cooked grits

plain breadcrumbs

oil for misting or cooking spray

honey or maple syrup for serving (optional)

1. While grits are still warm, spread them into a square or rectangular baking pan, about ½-inch thick. If your grits are thicker than that, scoop some out into another pan.

2. Chill several hours or overnight, until grits are cold and firm.

3. When ready to cook, pour off any water that has collected in pan and cut grits into 2- to 3-inch squares.

4. Dip grits squares in breadcrumbs and place in air fryer basket in single layer, close but not touching.

5. Cook at 390°F for 10 to 12 minutes, until heated through and crispy brown on the outside.

6. Serve while hot either plain or with a drizzle of honey or maple syrup.

Grits Casserole

Yield: 4 servings | Prep Time: 5 minutes | Cooking Time: asparagus 5 minutes, casserole 23–25 minutes | Total Time: 33–35 minutes

GLUTEN FREE

This versatile dish works well for breakfast, brunch, lunch, or dinner. We love it alongside a good steak.

10 fresh asparagus spears, cut into 1-inch pieces

2 cups cooked grits, cooled to room temperature

1 egg, beaten

2 teaspoons Worcestershire sauce

½ teaspoon garlic powder

¼ teaspoon salt

2 slices provolone cheese (about 1½ ounces)

oil for misting or cooking spray

1. Mist asparagus spears with oil and cook at 390°F for 5 minutes, until crisp-tender.

2. In a medium bowl, mix together the grits, egg, Worcestershire, garlic powder, and salt.

3. Spoon half of grits mixture into air fryer baking pan and top with asparagus.

4. Tear cheese slices into pieces and layer evenly on top of asparagus.

5. Top with remaining grits.

6. Bake at 360°F for 23 to 25 minutes. The casserole will rise a little as it cooks. When done, the top will have browned lightly with just a hint of crispiness.

Hasselbacks

Yield: 4 servings | Prep Time: 10 minutes | Cooking Time: 41 minutes | Total Time: 51 minutes

GLUTEN FREE   SUPER EASY   TASTER FAVORITE

These make a nice side for roast pork or beef as well as a main course for lunch. Either way, round out the meal with a simple tossed salad.

2 large potatoes (approx. 1 pound each)

oil for misting or cooking spray

salt, pepper, and garlic powder

1½ ounces sharp Cheddar cheese, sliced very thin

¼ cup chopped green onions

2 strips turkey bacon, cooked and crumbled

light sour cream for serving (optional)

1. Preheat air fryer to 390°F.

2. Scrub potatoes. Cut thin vertical slices ¼-inch thick crosswise about three-quarters of the way down so that bottom of potato remains intact.

3. Fan potatoes slightly to separate slices. Mist with oil and sprinkle with salt, pepper, and garlic powder to taste. Potatoes will be very stiff, but try to get some of the oil and seasoning between the slices.

4. Place potatoes in air fryer basket and cook for 40 minutes or until centers test done when pierced with a fork.

5. Top potatoes with cheese slices and cook for 30 seconds to 1 minute to melt cheese.

6. Cut each potato in half crosswise, and sprinkle with green onions and crumbled bacon. If you like, add a dollop of sour cream before serving.

Hawaiian Brown Rice

Yield: 4–6 servings | Prep Time: 10 minutes | Cooking Time: 12–16 minutes | Total Time: 22–26 minutes

GLUTEN FREE   TASTER FAVORITE

This unique side dish has a different but not overpowering taste. It perfectly complements a wide variety of foods, and the mild flavor even works well with spicy dishes.

¼ pound ground sausage

1 teaspoon butter

¼ cup minced onion

¼ cup minced bell pepper

2 cups cooked brown rice

1 8-ounce can crushed pineapple, drained

1. Shape sausage into 3 or 4 thin patties. Cook at 390°F for 6 to 8 minutes or until well done. Remove from air fryer, drain, and crumble. Set aside.

2. Place butter, onion, and bell pepper in baking pan. Cook at 390°F for 1 minute and stir. Cook 3 to 4 minutes longer or just until vegetables are tender.

3. Add sausage, rice, and pineapple to vegetables and stir together.

4. Cook at 390°F for 2 to 3 minutes, until heated through.

VARIATION: If pepper is your passion, try using spicy pork sausage for this recipe.

Home Fries

Yield: 3–4 servings | Prep Time: 8 minutes | Cooking Time: 20–25 minutes | Total Time: 28–33 minutes

GLUTEN FREE SUPER EASY VEGETARIAN

Is there ever a wrong meal for Home Fries? They go with practically everything. We love them alongside eggs for breakfast or with a good steak or pork chop for dinner.

3 pounds potatoes, cut into 1-inch cubes

½ teaspoon oil

salt and pepper

1. In a large bowl, mix the potatoes and oil thoroughly.

2. Cook at 390°F for 10 minutes and shake the basket to redistribute potatoes.

3. Cook for an additional 10 to 15 minutes, until brown and crisp.

4. Season with salt and pepper to taste.

Mashed Potato Tots

Yield: 18–24 tots | Prep Time: 20 minutes | Cooking Time: 10–12 minutes per batch | Total Time: 40–44 minutes

KID PLEASER

Stiff mashed potatoes work best in this recipe, so it helps to plan ahead. After you cook and mash your potatoes, scoop out 1 cup and set it aside before you add any thinners such as milk, butter, or sour cream. Refrigerate that reserved cup of potatoes and use them the next day to make these crispy tots. Using leftovers will cut your cooking time in half.

---

1 medium potato or 1 cup cooked mashed potatoes

1 tablespoon real bacon bits

2 tablespoons chopped green onions, tops only

1/4 teaspoon onion powder

1 teaspoon dried chopped chives

salt

2 tablespoons flour

1 egg white, beaten

1/2 cup panko breadcrumbs

oil for misting or cooking spray

NOTE: To double this recipe, double all ingredients, except instead of 2 egg whites, use 1 whole egg.

TIP: Coating the tots is easier than it sounds. Even stiff mashed potatoes are hard to shape by hand because they tend to stick to your fingers. Rather than touching them, touch the crumbs instead and use your fingers like little bulldozers to turn potatoes and gently push them into shape.

1. If using cooked mashed potatoes, jump to step 4.

2. Peel potato and cut into 1/2-inch cubes. (Small pieces cook more quickly.) Place in saucepan, add water to cover, and heat to boil. Lower heat slightly and continue cooking just until tender, about 10 minutes.

3. Drain potatoes and place in ice cold water. Allow to cool for a minute or two, then drain well and mash.

4. Preheat air fryer to 390°F.

5. In a large bowl, mix together the potatoes, bacon bits, onions, onion powder, chives, salt to taste, and flour. Add egg white and stir well.

6. Place panko crumbs on a sheet of wax paper.

7. For each tot, use about 2 teaspoons of potato mixture. To shape, drop the measure of potato mixture onto panko crumbs and push crumbs up and around potatoes to coat edges. Then turn tot over to coat other side with crumbs. (See tip.)

8. Mist tots with oil or cooking spray and place in air fryer basket, crowded but not stacked.

9. Cook at 390°F for 10 to 12 minutes, until browned and crispy.

10. Repeat steps 8 and 9 to cook remaining tots.

Mashed Sweet Potato Tots

Yield: 18–24 tots | Prep Time: 10 minutes | Cooking Time: 12–13 minutes per batch | Total Time: 34–36 minutes

KID PLEASER   VEGETARIAN

Traditional Thanksgiving sweet potato casseroles inspired this recipe. For our tots, we kept the good stuff and replaced all the processed sugar with just a touch of honey. Chopped pecans make the tots extra special.

---

1 cup cooked mashed sweet potatoes

1 egg white, beaten

$^1/_8$ teaspoon ground cinnamon

1 dash nutmeg

2 tablespoons chopped pecans

$1^1/_2$ teaspoons honey

salt

$^1/_2$ cup panko breadcrumbs

oil for misting or cooking spray

1. Preheat air fryer to 390°F.

2. In a large bowl, mix together the potatoes, egg white, cinnamon, nutmeg, pecans, honey, and salt to taste.

3. Place panko crumbs on a sheet of wax paper.

4. For each tot, use about 2 teaspoons of sweet potato mixture. To shape, drop the measure of potato mixture onto panko crumbs and push crumbs up and around potatoes to coat edges. Then turn tot over to coat other side with crumbs. (See tip on page 169.)

5. Mist tots with oil or cooking spray and place in air fryer basket in single layer.

6. Cook at 390°F for 12 to 13 minutes, until browned and crispy.

7. Repeat steps 5 and 6 to cook remaining tots.

> **NOTE:** To double this recipe, double all ingredients, except instead of 2 egg whites, use 1 whole egg.

Mushrooms

Yield: 4 servings | Prep Time: 10 minutes | Cooking Time: 12 minutes | Total Time: 22 minutes

TASTER FAVORITE VEGETARIAN

Cooking many foods with a high moisture content can prove challenging in an air fryer. Fried mushrooms are an exception. The coating contains panko for maximum crunch, and these taste *better* than the deep-fried version.

8 ounces whole white button mushrooms

½ teaspoon salt

⅛ teaspoon pepper

¼ teaspoon garlic powder

¼ teaspoon onion powder

5 tablespoons potato starch

1 egg, beaten

¾ cup panko breadcrumbs

oil for misting or cooking spray

1. Place mushrooms in a large bowl. Add the salt, pepper, garlic and onion powders, and stir well to distribute seasonings.

2. Add potato starch to mushrooms and toss in bowl until well coated.

3. Dip mushrooms in beaten egg, roll in panko crumbs, and mist with oil or cooking spray.

4. Place mushrooms in air fryer basket. You can cook them all at once, and it's okay if a few are stacked.

5. Cook at 390°F for 5 minutes. Shake basket, then continue cooking for 5 to 7 more minutes, until golden brown and crispy.

Mushrooms, Sautéed

Yield: 2–4 servings | Prep Time: 5 minutes | Cooking Time: 4–5 minutes | Total Time: 9–10 minutes

GLUTEN FREE   SUPER EASY

This recipe easily serves 4 when used as a topping for main dishes, such as Boneless Ribeyes (page 92). As a stand-alone side dish, it makes only 2 full servings, but you can double the recipe easily.

8 ounces sliced white mushrooms, rinsed and well drained

¼ teaspoon garlic powder

1 tablespoon Worcestershire sauce

1. Place mushrooms in a large bowl and sprinkle with garlic powder and Worcestershire. Stir well to distribute seasonings evenly.

2. Place in air fryer basket and cook at 390°F for 4 to 5 minutes, until tender.

Okra

Yield: 4 servings | Prep Time: 15 minutes | Cooking Time: 12–17 minutes | Total Time: 27–30 minutes

VEGETARIAN

Adding fried okra to a southern summer supper of fresh corn on the cob, purple hull peas, and sliced tomatoes makes an unbeatable meal, and the air fryer does an exceptionally good job with okra. If you're a fan of deep-fried okra, you're going to love this recipe!

7–8 ounces fresh okra

1 egg

1 cup milk

1 cup breadcrumbs

½ teaspoon salt

oil for misting or cooking spray

1. Remove stem ends from okra and cut in ½-inch slices.

2. In a medium bowl, beat together egg and milk. Add okra slices and stir to coat.

3. In a sealable plastic bag or container with lid, mix together the breadcrumbs and salt.

4. Remove okra from egg mixture, letting excess drip off, and transfer into bag with breadcrumbs.

5. Shake okra in crumbs to coat well.

6. Place all of the coated okra into the air fryer basket and mist with oil or cooking spray. Okra doesn't need to cook in a single layer, nor is it necessary to spray all sides at this point. A good spritz on top will do.

7. Cook at 390°F for 5 minutes. Shake basket to redistribute and give it another spritz as you shake.

8. Cook 5 more minutes. Shake and spray again. Cook for 2 to 5 minutes longer or until golden brown and crispy.

TIP: Make sure okra is well drained before placing it in the breadcrumbs. Use a slotted spoon to lift a little okra at a time and let plenty of the egg wash drip off before putting it into the breadcrumb mixture.

Onion Rings

Yield: 4 servings | Prep Time: 15 minutes | Cooking Time: 12–16 minutes | Total Time: 27–31 minutes

VEGETARIAN

You can't stack many foods in multiple layers in an air fryer because stacking blocks the air flow, which is vital to the cooking process. Onion rings are an exception. Even when they overlap, plenty of gaps allow for air circulation. See insert B8 for recipe photo.

---

1 large onion (preferably Vidalia or 1015)

½ cup flour, plus 2 tablespoons

½ teaspoon salt

½ cup beer, plus 2 tablespoons

1 cup crushed panko breadcrumbs

oil for misting or cooking spray

1. Peel onion, slice, and separate into rings.

2. In a large bowl, mix together the flour and salt. Add beer and stir until it stops foaming and makes a thick batter.

3. Place onion rings in batter and stir to coat.

4. Place breadcrumbs in a sealable plastic bag or container with lid.

5. Working with a few at a time, remove onion rings from batter, shaking off excess, and drop into breadcrumbs. Shake to coat, then lay out onion rings on cookie sheet or wax paper.

6. When finished, spray onion rings with oil or cooking spray and pile into air fryer basket.

7. Cook at 390°F for 5 minutes. Shake basket and mist with oil. Cook 5 minutes and mist again. Cook an additional 2 to 4 minutes, until golden brown and crispy.

Onions

Yield: 4 servings | Prep Time: 10 minutes | Cooking Time: 18–20 minutes | Total Time: 28–30 minutes

GLUTEN FREE   SUPER EASY   VEGETARIAN

Serve these as a side with grilled steak or barbecued meat. If you don't have Gruyère, substitute 1 ounce of blue cheese crumbles.

---

2 yellow onions (Vidalia or 1015 recommended)

salt and pepper

¼ teaspoon ground thyme

¼ teaspoon smoked paprika

2 teaspoons olive oil

1 ounce Gruyère cheese, grated

1. Peel onions and halve lengthwise (vertically).

2. Sprinkle cut sides of onions with salt, pepper, thyme, and paprika.

3. Place each onion half, cut-surface up, on a large square of aluminum foil. Pull sides of foil up to cup around onion. Drizzle cut surface of onions with oil.

4. Crimp foil at top to seal closed.

5. Place wrapped onions in air fryer basket and cook at 390°F for 18 to 20 minutes. When done, onions should be soft enough to pierce with fork but still slightly firm.

6. Open foil just enough to sprinkle each onion with grated cheese.

7. Cook for 30 seconds to 1 minute to melt cheese.

> **NOTE:** You need to leave plenty of space between the foil and the heating coils at the top of your air fryer. Use scissors or kitchen shears to cut off excess foil so it doesn't stand up too tall.

Polenta

Yield: 4 servings | Prep Time: 5 minutes | Cooking Time: 13–15 minutes | Total Time: 18–20 minutes

SUPER EASY   VEGETARIAN

Serve polenta alongside any kind of roast, including our Italian Tuna Roast (page 126). You also can use it as the base for creating other sides or even main dishes. Spoon sausage and peppers over it or cut cooked polenta slices into quarters and serve with marinara sauce for an easy game-day meal.

1 pound polenta

¼ cup flour

oil for misting or cooking spray

1. Cut polenta into ½-inch slices.

2. Dip slices in flour to coat well. Spray both sides with oil or cooking spray.

3. Cook at 390°F for 5 minutes. Turn polenta and spray both sides again with oil.

4. Cook 8 to 10 more minutes or until brown and crispy.

Rosemary New Potatoes

Yield: 4 servings | Prep Time: 10 minutes | Cooking Time: 5–6 minutes | Total Time: 15–16 minutes

GLUTEN FREE SUPER EASY VEGETARIAN

Any size potato will work for this recipe, so long as you end up with about 3 cups after slicing. You can slice small new potatoes as is to create little "rounds." For large red potatoes, cut each in half first, then cut each of the halves into 3/8-thick slices.

3 large red potatoes (enough to make 3 cups sliced)

1/4 teaspoon ground rosemary

1/4 teaspoon ground thyme

1/8 teaspoon salt

1/8 teaspoon ground black pepper

2 teaspoons extra-light olive oil

1. Preheat air fryer to 330°F.

2. Place potatoes in large bowl and sprinkle with rosemary, thyme, salt, and pepper.

3. Stir with a spoon to distribute seasonings evenly.

4. Add oil to potatoes and stir again to coat well.

5. Cook at 330°F for 4 minutes. Stir and break apart any that have stuck together.

6. Cook an additional 1 to 2 minutes or until fork-tender.

VARIATION: After cooking as above, these potatoes will be soft and tender. You can continue cooking for 5 to 8 more minutes, until potatoes begin to brown a little. They won't harden like chips, but the extra cooking time will add a slight crisp to the outside.

Stuffed Avocados

Yield: 4 avocado halves | Prep Time: 5 minutes | Cooking Time: 6–8 minutes | Total Time: 11–13 minutes

GLUTEN FREE   SUPER EASY   VEGETARIAN

Avocados are a nutritious fruit, full of healthy omega-3 fatty acids. Served for lunch or an afternoon snack, these stuffed avocados will help stave off hunger all afternoon.

---

1 cup frozen shoepeg corn, thawed

1 cup cooked black beans

1/4 cup diced onion

1/2 teaspoon cumin

2 teaspoons lime juice, plus extra for serving

salt and pepper

2 large avocados, split in half, pit removed

1. Mix together the corn, beans, onion, cumin, and lime juice. Season to taste with salt and pepper.

2. Scoop out some of the flesh from center of each avocado and set aside. Divide corn mixture evenly between the cavities.

3. Set avocado halves in air fryer basket and cook at 360°F for 6 to 8 minutes, until corn mixture is hot.

4. Season the avocado flesh that you scooped out with a squirt of lime juice, salt, and pepper. Spoon it over the cooked halves.

TIP: Leaving the skin on the avocados helps hold them together while cooking.

Sweet Potato Fries

Yield: 4 servings | Prep Time: 15 minutes | Cooking Time: 30 minutes | Total Time: 45 minutes

GLUTEN FREE   KID PLEASER   SUPER EASY   VEGETARIAN

These are a popular substitute for fries made with white potatoes. Marjoram amps up the flavor, but you can use whatever seasoning(s) you like. Experiment with hot or savory spices, such as curry powder or cinnamon, to discover delicious new flavor combinations.

---

2 pounds sweet potatoes

1 teaspoon dried marjoram

2 teaspoons olive oil

sea salt

1. Peel and cut the potatoes into ¼-inch sticks, 4 to 5 inches long.

2. In a sealable plastic bag or bowl with lid, toss sweet potatoes with marjoram and olive oil. Rub seasonings in to coat well.

3. Pour sweet potatoes into air fryer basket and cook at 390°F for approximately 30 minutes, until cooked through with some brown spots on edges.

4. Season to taste with sea salt.

TIP: Drizzle the fries with honey, sprinkle them with Sriracha, or top them with melted cheese. Go bold with dipping sauces. Try ranch dressing, honey mustard, aioli, sweet and sour sauce, or even flavored yogurt.

Yellow Squash

Yield: 4 servings | Prep Time: 20 minutes | Cooking Time: 10–12 minutes | Total Time: 30–32 minutes

VEGETARIAN

Coating the squash slices takes a little time, but it's well worth it. This healthier air-fryer version tastes every bit as good as deep-fried—if not better.

---

1 large yellow squash (about 1½ cups)

2 eggs

¼ cup buttermilk

1 cup panko breadcrumbs

¼ cup white cornmeal

½ teaspoon salt

oil for misting or cooking spray

1. Preheat air fryer to 390°F.

2. Cut the squash into ¼-inch slices.

3. In a shallow dish, beat together eggs and buttermilk.

4. In sealable plastic bag or container with lid, combine ¼ cup panko crumbs, white cornmeal, and salt. Shake to mix well.

5. Place the remaining ¾ cup panko crumbs in a separate shallow dish.

6. Dump all the squash slices into the egg/buttermilk mixture. Stir to coat.

7. Remove squash from buttermilk mixture with a slotted spoon, letting excess drip off, and transfer to the panko/cornmeal mixture. Close bag or container and shake well to coat.

8. Remove squash from crumb mixture, letting excess fall off. Return squash to egg/buttermilk mixture, stirring gently to coat. If you need more liquid to coat all the squash, add a little more buttermilk.

9. Remove each squash slice from egg wash and dip in a dish of ¾ cup panko crumbs.

10. Mist squash slices with oil or cooking spray and place in air fryer basket. Squash should be in a single layer, but it's okay if the slices crowd together and overlap a little.

11. Cook at 390°F for 5 minutes. Shake basket to break up any that have stuck together. Mist again with oil or spray.

12. Cook 5 minutes longer and check. If necessary, mist again with oil and cook an additional minute or two, until squash slices are golden brown and crisp.

SALADS

Chicken Salad with Sunny Citrus Dressing

Yield: 4 servings | Prep Time: 35 minutes | Cooking Time: 6–8 minutes | Total Time: 41–43 minutes

GLUTEN FREE

This salad makes a hearty main course, but omit the chicken and it becomes a delicious side salad.

Sunny Citrus Dressing

1 cup first cold-pressed extra virgin olive oil

⅓ cup red wine vinegar

2 tablespoons all natural orange marmalade

1 teaspoon dry mustard

1 teaspoon ground black pepper

California Chicken

4 large chicken tenders

1 teaspoon olive oil

juice of 1 small orange or clementine

salt and pepper

½ teaspoon rosemary

Salad

8 cups romaine or leaf lettuce, chopped or torn into bite-size pieces

2 clementines or small oranges, peeled and sectioned

½ cup dried cranberries

4 tablespoons sliced almonds

1. In a 2-cup jar or container with lid, combine all dressing ingredients and shake until well blended. Refrigerate for at least 30 minutes for flavors to blend.

2. Brush chicken tenders lightly with oil.

3. Drizzle orange juice over chicken.

4. Sprinkle with salt and pepper to taste.

5. Crush the rosemary and sprinkle over chicken.

6. Cook at 390°F for 3 minutes, turn over, and cook for an additional 3 to 5 minutes or until chicken is tender and juices run clear.

7. When ready to serve, toss lettuce with 2 tablespoons of dressing to coat.

8. Divide lettuce among 4 plates or bowls. Arrange chicken and clementines on top and sprinkle cranberries and almonds. Pass extra dressing at the table.

TIP: Fresh juice is always best, but you can substitute 1 tablespoon bottled orange juice for the fresh squeezed above.

Pork Tenderloin Salad

Yield: 4 servings | Prep Time: 15 minutes | Cooking Time: 25 minutes | Total Time: 40 minutes

GLUTEN FREE   SUPER EASY   TASTER FAVORITE

We love a good salad for dinner, but some of the meat lovers in our families aren't too crazy about eating a bowl of just lettuce and fresh veggies. This hearty salad will win them over with a generous serving of pork roast and healthy greens too.

Pork Tenderloin
½ teaspoon smoked paprika
¼ teaspoon salt
¼ teaspoon garlic powder
½ teaspoon onion powder
⅛ teaspoon ginger
1 teaspoon extra-light olive oil
¾ pound pork tenderloin

Dressing
3 tablespoons extra-light olive oil
2 tablespoons red wine vinegar
2 tablespoons Dijon mustard
1 tablespoon honey

Salad
¼ sweet red bell pepper
1 large Granny Smith apple
8 cups shredded Napa cabbage

1. Mix the tenderloin seasonings together with oil and rub all over surface of meat.

2. Place pork tenderloin in the air fryer basket and cook at 390°F for 25 minutes, until meat registers 130°F on a meat thermometer.

3. Allow meat to rest while preparing salad and dressing.

4. In a jar, shake all dressing ingredients together until well mixed.

5. Cut the bell pepper into slivers, then core, quarter, and slice the apple crosswise.

6. In a large bowl, toss together the cabbage, bell pepper, apple, and dressing.

7. Divide salad mixture among 4 plates.

8. Slice pork tenderloin into ½-inch slices and divide among the 4 salads.

9. Serve with sweet potato or other vegetable chips.

> **TIP:** Without the pork, the cabbage salad and dressing makes a great side for fried fish such as Catfish Nuggets or Almond-Crusted Fish (page 116). Try it intead of your usual coleslaw.

Salmon Salad with Steamboat Dressing

Yield: 4 servings | Prep Time: 40 minutes | Cooking Time: 15–18 minutes | Total Time: 55–58 minutes

GLUTEN FREE   SUPER EASY

This cool salad with heart-healthy salmon and delicious fresh asparagus is a wonderful way to welcome spring.

¼ teaspoon salt

1½ teaspoons dried dill weed

1 tablespoon fresh lemon juice

8 ounces fresh or frozen salmon fillet (skin on)

8 cups shredded romaine, Boston, or other leaf lettuce

8 spears cooked asparagus, cut in 1-inch pieces

8 cherry tomatoes, halved or quartered

1. Mix the salt and dill weed together. Rub the lemon juice over the salmon on both sides and sprinkle the dill and salt all over. Refrigerate for 15 to 20 minutes.

2. Make Steamboat Dressing (right) and refrigerate while cooking salmon and preparing salad.

3. Cook salmon in air fryer basket at 330°F for 15 to 18 minutes. Cooking time will vary depending on thickness of fillets. When done, salmon should flake with fork but still be moist and tender.

4. Remove salmon from air fryer and cool slightly. At this point, the skin should slide off easily. Cut salmon into 4 pieces and discard skin.

5. Divide the lettuce among 4 plates. Scatter asparagus spears and tomato pieces evenly over the lettuce, allowing roughly 2 whole spears and 2 whole cherry tomatoes per plate.

6. Top each salad with one portion of the salmon and drizzle with a tablespoon of dressing. Serve with additional dressing to pass at the table.

Steamboat Shrimp Salad

Yield: 4 servings | Prep Time: 25 minutes | Cooking Time: 4 minutes | Total Time: 29 minutes

GLUTEN FREE   TASTER FAVORITE

Do not use bottled lemon juice for the dressing below. Freshly squeezed juice gives it an extra-delicious burst of citrus flavor that a bottle can't match. Also, don't omit the hot sauce. It's a small amount, but it makes a big difference.

Steamboat Dressing

¹⁄₂ cup mayonnaise

¹⁄₂ cup plain yogurt

2 teaspoons freshly squeezed lemon juice (no substitutes)

2 teaspoons grated lemon rind

1 teaspoon dill weed, slightly crushed

¹⁄₂ teaspoon hot sauce

Steamed Shrimp

24 small, raw shrimp, peeled and deveined

1 teaspoon lemon juice

¹⁄₄ teaspoon Old Bay Seasoning

Salad

8 cups romaine or Bibb lettuce, chopped or torn

¹⁄₄ cup red onion, cut in thin slivers

12 black olives, sliced

12 cherry or grape tomatoes, halved

1 medium avocado, sliced or cut into large chunks

1. Combine all dressing ingredients and mix well. Refrigerate while preparing shrimp and salad.

2. Sprinkle raw shrimp with lemon juice and Old Bay Seasoning. Use more Old Bay if you like your shrimp bold and spicy.

3. Pour 4 tablespoons of water in bottom of air fryer.

4. Place shrimp in air fryer basket in single layer.

5. Cook at 390°F for 4 minutes. Remove shrimp from basket and place in refrigerator to cool.

6. Combine all salad ingredients and mix gently. Divide among 4 salad plates or bowls.

7. Top each salad with 6 shrimp and serve with dressing.

NOTE: We prefer Hellman's mayonnaise and Frank's RedHot Buffalo Wings Sauce for this recipe. We also like the above method for cooking shrimp because it's fast and they turn out moist, tender, and tasty. It's also the best choice if you're squeamish about cooking shrimp without deveining them first. Experts prefer steaming shrimp in the shell because it protects the delicate meat and ensures the best results. You can cook unpeeled shrimp in an air fryer, but that may require a little more cooking time. Watch closely, though, and take care not to overcook.

Tofu & Broccoli Salad

Yield: 4 servings | Prep Time: 50 minutes | Cooking Time: 17–20 minutes | Total Time: 67–70 minutes

GLUTEN FREE TASTER FAVORITE VEGETARIAN

Fried tofu works extremely well in an air fryer. The key is making sure it's well drained. Tofu presses are great for that, but we've included instructions if you don't own one.

Broccoli Salad

4 cups fresh broccoli, cut into bite-size pieces

½ cup red onion, chopped

⅓ cup raisins or dried cherries

¾ cup sliced almonds

½ cup Asian-style salad dressing

Tofu

4 ounces extra firm tofu

1 teaspoon smoked paprika

1 teaspoon onion powder

¼ teaspoon salt

2 tablespoons cornstarch

1 tablespoon extra virgin olive oil

1. Place several folded paper towels on a plate and set tofu on top. Cover tofu with another folded paper towel, put another plate on top, and add heavy items such as canned goods to weigh it down. Press tofu for 30 minutes.

2. While tofu is draining, combine all salad ingredients in a large bowl. Toss together well, cover, and chill until ready to serve.

3. Cut the tofu into small cubes, about ¼-inch thick. Sprinkle the cubes top and bottom with the paprika, onion powder, and salt.

4. Place cornstarch in small plastic bag, add tofu, and shake until cubes are well coated.

5. Place olive oil in another small plastic bag, add coated tofu, and shake to coat well.

6. Cook at 330°F for 17 to 20 minutes or until as crispy as you like.

7. To serve, stir chilled salad well, divide among 4 plates, and top with fried tofu.

TIP: We recommend Newman's Own Sesame Ginger Dressing for this recipe.

Tuna Platter

Yield: 4–6 servings | Prep Time: 20 minutes | Cooking Time: 7–9 minutes | Total Time: 27–29 minutes

GLUTEN FREE

Channel your inner artist as you arrange the ingredients for this delicious and healthy main-dish salad.

4 new potatoes, boiled in their jackets

½ cup vinaigrette dressing, plus 2 tablespoons

½ pound fresh green beans, cut in half-inch pieces and steamed

1 tablespoon Herbes de Provence

1 tablespoon minced shallots

1½ tablespoons tarragon vinegar

4 tuna steaks, each ¾-inch thick, about 1 pound

salt and pepper

Salad

8 cups chopped romaine lettuce

12 grape tomatoes, halved lengthwise

½ cup pitted olives (black, green, nicoise, or combination)

2 boiled eggs, peeled and halved lengthwise

1. Quarter potatoes and toss with 1 tablespoon salad dressing.

2. Toss the warm beans with the other tablespoon of salad dressing. Set both aside while you prepare the tuna.

3. Mix together the herbs, shallots, and vinegar and rub into all sides of tuna. Season fish to taste with salt and pepper.

4. Cook tuna at 390°F for 7 minutes and check. If needed, cook 1 to 2 minutes longer, until tuna is barely pink in the center.

5. Spread the lettuce over a large platter.

6. Slice the tuna steaks in ½-inch pieces and arrange them in the center of the lettuce.

7. Place the remaining ingredients around the tuna. Diners create their own plates by selecting what they want from the platter. Pass remainder of salad dressing at the table.

TIP: We recommend Newman's Own Olive Oil & Vinegar salad dressing for this recipe.

BREADS

Banana Bread

Yield: 1 loaf (approx. 6–8 servings) | Prep Time: 5 minutes | Cooking Time: 20 minutes | Total Time: 25 minutes

KID PLEASER   SUPER EASY   VEGETARIAN

Making healthier banana bread is easy. We use whole-grain flour, no added sugar, and just a little maple syrup to enhance the bananas' natural sweetness.

cooking spray

1 cup white wheat flour

$\frac{1}{2}$ teaspoon baking powder

$\frac{1}{4}$ teaspoon salt

$\frac{1}{4}$ teaspoon baking soda

1 egg

$\frac{1}{2}$ cup mashed ripe banana

$\frac{1}{4}$ cup plain yogurt

$\frac{1}{4}$ cup pure maple syrup

2 tablespoons coconut oil

$\frac{1}{2}$ teaspoon pure vanilla extract

1. Preheat air fryer to 330°F.

2. Lightly spray 6 x 6-inch baking dish with cooking spray.

3. In a medium bowl, mix together the flour, baking powder, salt, and soda.

4. In a separate bowl, beat the egg and add the mashed banana, yogurt, syrup, oil, and vanilla. Mix until well combined.

5. Pour liquid mixture into dry ingredients and stir gently to blend. Do not beat. Batter may be slightly lumpy.

6. Pour batter into baking dish and cook at 330°F for 20 minutes or until toothpick inserted in center of loaf comes out clean.

Broccoli Cornbread

Yield: 1 loaf (approx. 6–8 servings) | Prep Time: 10 minutes | Cooking Time: 18–20 minutes | Total Time: 28–30 minutes

SUPER EASY   VEGETARIAN

This cornbread is so moist that when it's warm you almost have to eat it with a fork. It goes great with most any kind of soup, especially tomato.

---

1 cup frozen chopped broccoli, thawed and drained

¼ cup cottage cheese

1 egg, beaten

2 tablespoons minced onion

2 tablespoons melted butter

½ cup flour

½ cup yellow cornmeal

1 teaspoon baking powder

½ teaspoon salt

¼ cup milk, plus 2 tablespoons

cooking spray

1. Place thawed broccoli in colander and press with a spoon to squeeze out excess moisture.

2. Stir together all ingredients in a large bowl.

3. Spray 6 x 6-inch baking pan with cooking spray.

4. Spread batter in pan and cook at 330°F for 18 to 20 minutes or until cornbread is lightly browned and loaf starts to pull away from sides of pan.

NOTE: After thawing and draining broccoli, you will have about ½ cup. Drain the broccoli especially well because too much moisture can prevent the cornbread from cooking completely through in the center.

Buttermilk Biscuits

Yield: 4 servings | Prep Time: 10 minutes | Cooking Time: 9–11 minutes | Total Time: 19–21 minutes

SUPER EASY   VEGETARIAN

In our grandmothers' day, buttermilk biscuits were an everyday staple. People ate them for breakfast, lunch, dinner, and snacks. They were made with pure lard and smothered with anything from sugary preserves to fattening white gravy. These days, biscuits have become a comfort food reserved for special occasions. Our version is a bit lighter, and they're perfectly delicious with nothing more than a drizzle of honey. This recipe makes enough for just one meal so you can't overindulge.

1 cup flour

1½ teaspoons baking powder

¼ teaspoon baking soda

¼ teaspoon salt

¼ cup butter, cut into tiny cubes

¼ cup buttermilk, plus 2 tablespoons

cooking spray

1. Preheat air fryer to 330°F.

2. Combine flour, baking powder, soda, and salt in a medium bowl. Stir together.

3. Add cubed butter and cut into flour using knives or a pastry blender.

4. Add buttermilk and stir into a stiff dough.

5. Divide dough into 4 portions and shape each into a large biscuit. If dough is too sticky to handle, stir in 1 or 2 more tablespoons of flour before shaping. Biscuits should be firm enough to hold their shape. Otherwise they will stick to the air fryer basket.

6. Spray air fryer basket with nonstick cooking spray.

7. Place biscuits in basket and cook at 330°F for 9 to 11 minutes.

Christmas Eggnog Bread

Yield: 1 loaf (approx. 6–8 servings) | Prep Time: 10 minutes | Cooking Time: 18–20 minutes | Total Time: 28–30 minutes

VEGETARIAN

This bread isn't overly sweet, and it has just enough candied fruit to give it a holiday look and taste without the heaviness of traditional fruitcake. It is best when eaten within a day, but if you have leftovers, try it sliced and toasted.

1 cup flour, plus more for dusting

¼ cup sugar

1 teaspoon baking powder

¼ teaspoon salt

¼ teaspoon nutmeg

½ cup eggnog

1 egg yolk

1 tablespoon butter, plus 1 teaspoon, melted

¼ cup pecans

¼ cup chopped candied fruit (cherries, pineapple, or mixed fruits)

cooking spray

1. Preheat air fryer to 360°F.

2. In a medium bowl, stir together the flour, sugar, baking powder, salt, and nutmeg.

3. Add eggnog, egg yolk, and butter. Mix well but do not beat.

4. Stir in nuts and fruit.

5. Spray a 6 x 6-inch baking pan with cooking spray and dust with flour.

6. Spread batter into prepared pan and cook at 360°F for 18 to 20 minutes or until top is dark golden brown and bread starts to pull away from sides of pan.

Cinnamon Biscuit Rolls

Yield: 12 rolls | Prep Time: 45 minutes | Cooking Time: 5–6 minutes per batch | Total Time: 55–57 minutes

KID PLEASER   TASTER FAVORITE   VEGETARIAN

These rolls come from a cross between yeast and biscuit dough. They require only one 30-minute rising, and they bake very quickly in an air fryer. You save time and still enjoy a taste very close to a traditional yeast roll.

Dough
¼ cup warm water (105–115°F)

1 teaspoon active dry yeast

1 tablespoon sugar

½ cup buttermilk, lukewarm

2 cups flour, plus more for dusting

1 teaspoon baking powder

½ teaspoon salt

3 tablespoons cold butter

Filling
1 tablespoon butter, melted

1 teaspoon cinnamon

2 tablespoons sugar

Icing
⅔ cup powdered sugar

¼ teaspoon vanilla

2–3 teaspoons milk

1. Dissolve yeast and sugar in warm water. Add buttermilk, stir, and set aside.

2. In a large bowl, sift together flour, baking powder, and salt. Using knives or a pastry blender, cut in butter until mixture is well combined and crumbly.

3. Pour in buttermilk mixture and stir with fork until a ball of dough forms.

4. Knead dough on a lightly floured surface for 5 minutes. Roll into an 8 x 11-inch rectangle.

5. For the filling, spread the melted butter over the dough.

6. In a small bowl, stir together the cinnamon and sugar, then sprinkle over dough.

7. Starting on a long side, roll up dough so that you have a roll about 11 inches long. Cut into 12 slices with a serrated knife and sawing motion so slices remain round.

8. Place rolls on a plate or cookie sheet about an inch apart and let rise for 30 minutes.

9. For icing, mix the powdered sugar, vanilla, and milk. Stir and add additional milk until icing reaches a good spreading consistency.

10. Preheat air fryer to 360°F.

11. Place 6 cinnamon rolls in basket and cook 5 to 6 minutes or until top springs back when lightly touched. Repeat to cook remaining 6 rolls.

12. Spread icing over warm rolls and serve.

Fry Bread

Yield: 4 servings | Prep Time: 15 minutes | Cooking Time: 5 minutes | Total Time: 20 minutes

SUPER EASY   VEGETARIAN

Eat this Native American fry bread as you would any flatbread. We like it made into tacos topped with beans, beef, cheese, chiles, lettuce, and tomato.

---

1 cup flour

2 teaspoons baking powder

¼ teaspoon salt

¼ cup lukewarm milk

1 teaspoon oil

2–3 tablespoons water

oil for misting or cooking spray

1. Stir together flour, baking powder, and salt. Gently mix in the milk and oil. Stir in 1 tablespoon water. If needed, add more water 1 tablespoon at a time until stiff dough forms. Dough shouldn't be sticky, so use only as much as you need.

2. Divide dough into 4 portions and shape into balls. Cover with a towel and let rest for 10 minutes.

3. Preheat air fryer to 390°F.

4. Shape dough as desired:

   a. Pat into 3-inch circles. This will make a thicker bread to eat plain or with a sprinkle of cinnamon or honey butter. You can cook all 4 at once.

   b. Pat thinner into rectangles about 3 x 6 inches. This will create a thinner bread to serve as a base for dishes such as Indian tacos. The circular shape is more traditional, but rectangles allow you to cook 2 at a time in your air fryer basket.

5. Spray both sides of dough pieces with oil or cooking spray.

6. Place the 4 circles or 2 of the dough rectangles in the air fryer basket and cook at 390°F for 3 minutes. Spray tops, turn, spray other side, and cook for 2 more minutes. If necessary, repeat to cook remaining bread.

7. Serve piping hot as is or allow to cool slightly and add toppings to create your own Native American tacos.

Garlic-Cheese Biscuits

Yield: 8 biscuits | Prep Time: 10 minutes | Cooking Time: 8–10 minutes | Total Time: 18–20 minutes

SUPER EASY   VEGETARIAN

Garlic adds a nice zip and takes these biscuits up a notch in flavor. If garlic isn't your thing, feel free to omit it, but the result may taste a little bland. Browse through your spice cabinet for any flavor that appeals to your taste.

1 cup self-rising flour

1 teaspoon garlic powder

2 tablespoons butter, diced

2 ounces sharp Cheddar cheese, grated

½ cup milk

cooking spray

1. Preheat air fryer to 330°F.

2. Combine flour and garlic in a medium bowl and stir together.

3. Using a pastry blender or knives, cut butter into dry ingredients.

4. Stir in cheese.

5. Add milk and stir until stiff dough forms.

6. If dough is too sticky to handle, stir in 1 or 2 more tablespoons of self-rising flour before shaping. Biscuits should be firm enough to hold their shape. Otherwise, they'll stick to the air fryer basket.

7. Divide dough into 8 portions and shape into 2-inch biscuits about ¾-inch thick.

8. Spray air fryer basket with nonstick cooking spray.

9. Place all 8 biscuits in basket and cook at 330°F for 8 to 10 minutes.

Pumpkin Loaf

Yield: 1 loaf (approx. 6–8 servings) | Prep Time: 10 minutes | Cooking Time: 22–25 minutes | Total Time: 32–35 minutes

SUPER EASY   VEGETARIAN

Each fall, you have to have a good slice of pumpkin bread at least once. It goes so well with a mug of hot apple cider, especially in front of a crackling fire.

cooking spray

1 large egg

½ cup granulated sugar

⅓ cup oil

½ cup canned pumpkin (*not* pie filling)

½ teaspoon vanilla

⅔ cup flour plus 1 tablespoon

½ teaspoon baking powder

½ teaspoon baking soda

½ teaspoon salt

1 teaspoon pumpkin pie spice

¼ teaspoon cinnamon

1. Spray 6 x 6-inch baking dish lightly with cooking spray.

2. Place baking dish in air fryer basket and preheat air fryer to 330°F.

3. In a large bowl, beat eggs and sugar together with a hand mixer.

4. Add oil, pumpkin, and vanilla and mix well.

5. Sift together all dry ingredients. Add to pumpkin mixture and beat well, about 1 minute.

6. Pour batter in baking dish and cook at 330°F for 22 to 25 minutes or until toothpick inserted in center of loaf comes out clean.

Scones

Yield: 9 scones | Prep Time: 10 minutes | Cooking Time: 6–8 minutes per batch | Total Time: 22–26 minutes

KID PLEASER   SUPER EASY   TASTER FAVORITE   VEGETARIAN

These dessert-size scones are a pure guilty pleasure yet super simple to make. They need no topping, filling, or even a dab of butter. They're perfectly delicious plain, especially piping hot right out of the air fryer.

2 cups self-rising flour, plus ¼ cup for kneading

⅓ cup granulated sugar

¼ cup butter, cold

1 cup milk

1. Preheat air fryer at 360°F.
2. In large bowl, stir together flour and sugar.
3. Cut cold butter into tiny cubes, and stir into flour mixture with fork.
4. Stir in milk until soft dough forms.
5. Sprinkle ¼ cup of flour onto wax paper and place dough on top. Knead lightly by folding and turning the dough about 6 to 8 times.
6. Pat dough into a 6 x 6-inch square.
7. Cut into 9 equal squares.
8. Place all squares in air fryer basket or as many as will fit in a single layer, close together but not touching.
9. Cook at 360°F for 6 to 8 minutes. When done, scones will be lightly browned on top and will spring back when pressed gently with a dull knife.
10. Repeat steps 8 and 9 to cook remaining scones.

> **TIP:** Knead very lightly. Overdoing it will make your scones turn out heavy.

Southern Sweet Cornbread

Yield: 6–8 servings | Prep Time: 5 minutes | Cooking Time: 17–19 minutes | Total Time: 22–24 minutes

SUPER EASY   VEGETARIAN

For a more traditional taste, omit the sugar. Either way, this cornbread is light and tender inside with a crunchy brown crust. See insert A8 for recipe photo.

---

cooking spray

½ cup white cornmeal

½ cup flour

2 teaspoons baking powder

½ teaspoon salt

4 teaspoons sugar

1 egg

2 tablespoons oil

½ cup milk

1. Preheat air fryer to 360°F.

2. Spray air fryer baking pan with nonstick cooking spray.

3. In a medium bowl, stir together the cornmeal, flour, baking powder, salt, and sugar.

4. In a small bowl, beat together the egg, oil, and milk. Stir into dry ingredients until well combined.

5. Pour batter into prepared baking pan.

6. Cook at 360°F for 17 to 19 minutes or until toothpick inserted in center comes out clean or with crumbs clinging.

Southwest Cornbread

Yield: 6–8 servings | Prep Time: 10 minutes | Cooking Time: 18–20 minutes | Total Time: 28–30 minutes

SUPER EASY   VEGETARIAN

Enjoy this versatile cornbread year-round. It makes the perfect partner for a hot bowl of chili on a cold winter night. In the heat of summer, it works equally well with a cool salad for a light lunch.

cooking spray

½ cup yellow cornmeal

½ cup flour

2 teaspoons baking powder

½ teaspoon salt

½ cup frozen corn kernels, thawed and drained

¼ cup finely chopped onion

1 or 2 small jalapeño peppers, seeded and chopped

1 egg

½ cup milk

2 tablespoons melted butter

2 ounces sharp Cheddar cheese, grated

1. Preheat air fryer to 360°F.

2. Spray air fryer baking pan with nonstick cooking spray.

3. In a medium bowl, stir together the cornmeal, flour, baking powder, and salt.

4. Stir in the corn, onion, and peppers.

5. In a small bowl, beat together the egg, milk, and butter. Stir into dry ingredients until well combined.

6. Spoon half the batter into prepared baking pan, spreading to edges. Top with grated cheese. Spoon remaining batter on top of cheese and gently spread to edges of pan so it completely covers the cheese.

7. Cook at 360°F for 18 to 20 minutes, until cornbread is done and top is crispy brown.

Strawberry Bread

Yield: 1 loaf (approx. 6–8 servings) | Prep Time: 10 minutes | Cooking Time: 28–30 minutes | Total Time: 38–40 minutes

KID PLEASER   VEGETARIAN

You can find the strawberries for this recipe in your grocer's freezer section, but don't drain them. Yes, it's decadent, but using both the fruit and the sweetened juice gives this bread maximum strawberry flavor. Make it a treat—not a habit!

½ cup frozen strawberries in juice, completely thawed (do not drain)

1 cup flour

½ cup sugar

1 teaspoon cinnamon

½ teaspoon baking soda

⅛ teaspoon salt

1 egg, beaten

⅓ cup oil

cooking spray

1. Cut any large berries into smaller pieces no larger than ½ inch.

2. Preheat air fryer to 330°F.

3. In a large bowl, stir together the flour, sugar, cinnamon, soda, and salt.

4. In a small bowl, mix together the egg, oil, and strawberries. Add to dry ingredients and stir together gently.

5. Spray 6 x 6-inch baking pan with cooking spray.

6. Pour batter into prepared pan and cook at 330°F for 28 to 30 minutes.

7. When bread is done, let cool for 10 minutes before removing from pan.

TIP: Serve this bread warm, cool, or sliced and toasted. For a little more crunch, add ½ cup of coconut or your favorite nuts to the batter.

Tuscan Toast

Yield: 4 servings | Prep Time: 10 minutes | Cooking Time: 5 minutes | Total Time: 15 minutes

SUPER EASY   VEGETARIAN

The garlic butter spread in this recipe tastes even better when you make it the day before and let the flavors meld in the fridge overnight. Make double, triple, or quadruple the spread and try it on baked potatoes, steamed broccoli, and lots of other vegetables.

$\frac{1}{4}$ cup butter

$\frac{1}{2}$ teaspoon lemon juice

$\frac{1}{2}$ clove garlic

$\frac{1}{2}$ teaspoon dried parsley flakes

4 slices Italian bread, 1-inch thick

1. Place butter, lemon juice, garlic, and parsley in a food processor. Process about 1 minute, or until garlic is pulverized and ingredients are well blended.

2. Spread garlic butter on both sides of bread slices.

3. Place bread slices upright in air fryer basket. (They can lie flat but cook better standing on end.)

4. Cook at 390°F for 5 minutes or until toasty brown.

TIP: If you don't have a food processor or the bowl is too large to process such a small amount, you can make the spread by hand. Finely mince the garlic, allow butter to soften to room temperature, then stir all ingredients together until well mixed.

White Wheat Walnut Bread

Yield: 8 servings | Prep Time: 25 minutes | Cooking Time: 20–25 minutes | Total Time: 45–50 minutes

TASTER FAVORITE   VEGETARIAN

The yeast for this bread comes in a ¾-ounce package containing three packets that are ¼ ounce each. You need only one packet. White wheat flour produces a lighter texture than the most commonly used whole wheat flour.

---

1 cup lukewarm water (105–115°F)

1 packet RapidRise yeast

1 tablespoon light brown sugar

2 cups whole-grain white wheat flour

1 egg, room temperature, beaten with a fork

2 teaspoons olive oil

½ teaspoon salt

½ cup chopped walnuts

cooking spray

1. In a small bowl, mix the water, yeast, and brown sugar.

2. Pour yeast mixture over flour and mix until smooth.

3. Add the egg, olive oil, and salt and beat with a wooden spoon for 2 minutes.

4. Stir in chopped walnuts. You will have very thick batter rather than stiff bread dough.

5. Spray air fryer baking pan with cooking spray and pour in batter, smoothing the top.

6. Let batter rise for 15 minutes.

7. Preheat air fryer to 360°F.

8. Cook bread for 20 to 25 minutes, until toothpick pushed into center comes out with crumbs clinging. Let bread rest for 10 minutes before removing from pan.

NOTE: Most whole wheat flour is ground from red wheat, which makes very dense bread. White wheat flour comes from white wheat, which gives a lighter color and milder taste. It also holds up better when rising.

Whole-Grain Cornbread

Yield: 6–8 servings | Prep Time: 5 minutes | Cooking Time: 25–30 minutes | Total Time: 30–35 minutes

GLUTEN FREE   SUPER EASY   TASTER FAVORITE   VEGETARIAN

This recipe makes a dense cornbread with lots of flavor. Enjoy the leftovers for breakfast as our grandparents did—covered in ice cold milk or buttermilk and eaten like a cereal.

1 cup stoneground cornmeal

$\frac{1}{2}$ cup brown rice flour

1 teaspoon sugar

2 teaspoons baking powder

$\frac{1}{4}$ teaspoon salt

1 cup milk

2 tablespoons oil

2 eggs

cooking spray

1. Preheat the air fryer to 360°F.

2. In a medium mixing bowl, mix cornmeal, brown rice flour, sugar, baking powder, and salt together.

3. Add the remaining ingredients and beat with a spoon until batter is smooth.

4. Spray air fryer baking pan with nonstick cooking spray and add the cornbread batter.

5. Bake at 360°F for 25 to 30 minutes, until center is done.

DESSERTS

Almond-Roasted Pears

Yield: 4 servings | Prep Time: 10 minutes | Cooking Time: 15–20 minutes | Total Time: 25–35 minutes

SUPER EASY TASTER FAVORITE VEGETARIAN

If you're looking for a light dessert, this is our favorite. It tastes absolutely delicious, but there's nothing terribly fattening here!

Yogurt Topping
1 container vanilla Greek yogurt (5–6 ounces)
¼ teaspoon almond flavoring

2 whole pears
¼ cup crushed Biscoff cookies (approx. 4 cookies)
1 tablespoon sliced almonds
1 tablespoon butter

1. Stir almond flavoring into yogurt and set aside while preparing pears.

2. Halve each pear and spoon out the core.

3. Place pear halves in air fryer basket.

4. Stir together the cookie crumbs and almonds. Place a quarter of this mixture into the hollow of each pear half.

5. Cut butter into 4 pieces and place one piece on top of crumb mixture in each pear.

6. Cook at 360°F for 15 to 20 minutes or until pears have cooked through but are still slightly firm.

7. Serve pears warm with a dollop of yogurt topping.

Apple Crisp

Yield: 4–6 servings | Prep Time: 10 minutes | Cooking Time: 16–18 minutes | Total Time: 26–28 minutes

GLUTEN FREE VEGETARIAN

Quinoa and oat bran give the crumb topping a wonderful crunch, a slightly different taste, and a bit of fiber. We've kept the sugar to a minimum, so enjoy this dessert without all the guilt.

Filling

3 Granny Smith apples, thinly sliced (about 4 cups)

¼ teaspoon ground cinnamon

⅛ teaspoon salt

1½ teaspoons lemon juice

2 tablespoons honey

1 tablespoon brown sugar

cooking spray

Crumb Topping

2 tablespoons oats

2 tablespoons oat bran

2 tablespoons cooked quinoa

2 tablespoons chopped walnuts

2 tablespoons brown sugar

2 teaspoons coconut oil

1. Combine all filling ingredients and stir well so that apples are evenly coated.

2. Spray air fryer baking pan with nonstick cooking spray and spoon in the apple mixture.

3. Cook at 360°F for 5 minutes. Stir well, scooping up from the bottom to mix apples and sauce.

4. At this point, the apples should be crisp-tender. Continue cooking in 3-minute intervals until apples are as soft as you like.

5. While apples are cooking, combine all topping ingredients in a small bowl. Stir until coconut oil mixes in well and distributes evenly. If your coconut oil is cold, it may be easier to mix in by hand.

6. When apples are cooked to your liking, sprinkle crumb mixture on top. Cook at 360°F for 8 to 10 minutes or until crumb topping is golden brown and crispy.

Baked Apple

Yield: 6 apple halves | Prep Time: 10 minutes | Cooking Time: 20 minutes | Total Time: 30 minutes

GLUTEN FREE   KID PLEASER   SUPER EASY   VEGETARIAN

When the weather starts to cool in autumn, we crave baked apples. Enjoy them as a nice light dessert, a breakfast treat alongside warm oatmeal, or garnish for a platter of roast pork.

3 small Honey Crisp or other baking apples

3 tablespoons maple syrup

3 tablespoons chopped pecans

1 tablespoon firm butter, cut into 6 pieces

1. Put ½ cup water in the drawer of the air fryer.

2. Wash apples well and dry them.

3. Split apples in half. Remove core and a little of the flesh to make a cavity for the pecans.

4. Place apple halves in air fryer basket, cut side up.

5. Spoon 1½ teaspoons pecans into each cavity.

6. Spoon ½ tablespoon maple syrup over pecans in each apple.

7. Top each apple with ½ teaspoon butter.

8. Cook at 360°F for 20 minutes, until apples are tender.

TIP: When done, lift the apples from the pan carefully, as they will be very hot.

Brownies After Dark

Yield: 4 servings | Prep Time: 10 minutes | Cooking Time: 11–13 minutes | Total Time: 21–23 minutes

KID PLEASER   SUPER EASY   TASTER FAVORITE   VEGETARIAN

If you don't love dark chocolate—and we mean *really* love it—this isn't the treat for you. For the rest of us, every bite of these brownies tastes like a chunk of heaven.

1 egg

½ cup granulated sugar

¼ teaspoon salt

½ teaspoon vanilla

¼ cup butter, melted

¼ cup flour, plus 2 tablespoons

¼ cup cocoa

cooking spray

Optional

vanilla ice cream

caramel sauce

whipped cream

1. Beat together egg, sugar, salt, and vanilla until light.

2. Add melted butter and mix well.

3. Stir in flour and cocoa.

4. Spray 6 x 6-inch baking pan lightly with cooking spray.

5. Spread batter in pan and cook at 330°F for 11 to 13 minutes. Cool and cut into 4 large squares or 16 small brownie bites.

TIP: For a truly indulgent dessert, cut the cooked brownie into 4 large squares and top with 1 scoop vanilla ice cream, caramel sauce, and whipped cream.

Chocolate Cake

Yield: 8 servings | Prep Time: 10 minutes | Cooking Time: 20–23 minutes | Total Time: 30–33 minutes

KID PLEASER   SUPER EASY   VEGETARIAN

This cake is delicious when served perfectly plain, especially while still warm. For a fancier presentation or to stretch it to serve more, top cake slices with whipped cream and fresh pitted cherries.

½ cup sugar

¼ cup flour, plus 3 tablespoons

3 tablespoons cocoa

½ teaspoon baking powder

½ teaspoon baking soda

¼ teaspoon salt

1 egg

2 tablespoons oil

½ cup milk

½ teaspoon vanilla extract

1. Preheat air fryer to 330°F.

2. Grease and flour a 6 x 6-inch baking pan.

3. In a medium bowl, stir together the sugar, flour, cocoa, baking powder, baking soda, and salt.

4. Add all other ingredients and beat with a wire whisk until smooth.

5. Pour batter into prepared pan and bake at 330°F for 20 to 23 minutes, until toothpick inserted in center comes out clean or with crumbs clinging to it.

Coconut-Custard Pie

Yield: 4 servings | Prep Time: 10 minutes | Cooking Time: 20–23 minutes | Total Time: 30–33 minutes

SUPER EASY   VEGETARIAN

This super easy pie forms just a hint of a crust on the bottom as it cooks. You can whip up this creamy dessert in just a few minutes. Serve it while still slightly warm or cold from the fridge.

1 cup milk

¼ cup plus 2 tablespoons sugar

¼ cup biscuit baking mix

1 teaspoon vanilla

2 eggs

2 tablespoons melted butter

cooking spray

½ cup shredded, sweetened coconut

1. Place all ingredients except coconut in a medium bowl.
2. Using a hand mixer, beat on high speed for 3 minutes.
3. Let sit for 5 minutes.
4. Preheat air fryer to 330°F.
5. Spray a 6-inch round or 6 x 6-inch square baking pan with cooking spray and place pan in air fryer basket.
6. Pour filling into pan and sprinkle coconut over top.
7. Cook pie at 330°F for 20 to 23 minutes or until center sets.

Coconut Macaroons

Yield: 12 macaroons | Prep Time: 5 minutes | Cooking Time: 8–10 minutes | Total Time: 13–15 minutes

SUPER EASY   TASTER FAVORITE   VEGETARIAN

Store these cookies in a tightly sealed bag or container so they stay nice and crispy. For an easy dessert, serve a macaroon with a scoop of peach or cherry sorbet on the side.

1⅓ cups shredded, sweetened coconut

4½ teaspoons flour

2 tablespoons sugar

1 egg white

½ teaspoon almond extract

1. Preheat air fryer to 330°F.
2. Mix all ingredients together.
3. Shape coconut mixture into 12 balls.
4. Place all 12 macaroons in air fryer basket. They won't expand, so you can place them close together, but they shouldn't touch.
5. Cook at 330°F for 8 to 10 minutes, until golden.

Coconut Rice Cake

Yield: 8 servings | Prep Time: 8 minutes | Cooking Time: 30–35 minutes | Total Time: 38–43 minutes

GLUTEN FREE SUPER EASY VEGETARIAN

This recipe makes a beautiful presentation for dessert because it molds and slices like a dream. For both looks and taste, we favor a combination of strawberry halves, fresh pineapple chunks, and sliced kiwi scattered around the cake.

1 cup all-natural coconut water

1 cup unsweetened coconut milk

1 teaspoon almond extract

1/4 teaspoon salt

4 tablespoons honey

cooking spray

3/4 cup raw jasmine rice

2 cups sliced or cubed fruit

1. In a medium bowl, mix together the coconut water, coconut milk, almond extract, salt, and honey.

2. Spray air fryer baking pan with cooking spray and add the rice.

3. Pour liquid mixture over rice.

4. Cook at 360°F for 15 minutes. Stir and cook for 15 to 20 minutes longer or until rice grains are tender.

5. Allow cake to cool slightly. Run a dull knife around edge of cake, inside the pan. Turn the cake out onto a platter and garnish with fruit.

Custard

Yield: 4–6 servings | Prep Time: 8 minutes | Cooking Time: 45–60 minutes | Total Time: 53–68 minutes

GLUTEN FREE **KID PLEASER** **SUPER EASY** **VEGETARIAN**

Custard may date as far back as Ancient Rome, and in recent decades it has become a favorite comfort-food dessert. Maybe that's because it's super easy to make and very economical. It's also the perfect light treat when you want something sweet but not too heavy.

---

2 cups whole milk

2 eggs

¼ cup sugar

⅛ teaspoon salt

¼ teaspoon vanilla

cooking spray

⅛ teaspoon nutmeg

1. In a blender, process milk, egg, sugar, salt, and vanilla until smooth.

2. Spray a 6 x 6-inch baking pan with nonstick spray and pour the custard into it.

3. Cook at 300°F for 45 to 60 minutes. Custard is done when the center sets.

4. Sprinkle top with the nutmeg.

5. Allow custard to cool slightly.

6. Serve it warm, at room temperature, or chilled.

TIP: Discard any liquid that accumulates in the pan after the custard is done. For a more colorful presentation, garnish your custard with fresh or stewed berries or sliced fruits.

Lamb Chops, page 99

Pork Loin, page 108

Pork Chops, page 106

Catfish Nuggets, page 118

Avocado Fries, page 28

Shrimp, page 131

Salmon, page 128

Fish Sticks for Grown-ups, page 122

Fish Tacos with Jalapeño-Lime Sauce, page 124

French Fries, page 161

Fried Oreos

Yield: 12 cookies | Prep Time: 7 minutes | Cooking Time: 6 minutes per batch | Total Time: 25 minutes

KID PLEASER   SUPER EASY   TASTER FAVORITE   VEGETARIAN

These delectable treats are great for bake sales, parties, and other events. Our version bakes for a lower-fat treat. After his first bite, our teenage taster responded with a resounding "Yes!"

---

oil for misting or nonstick spray

1 cup complete pancake and waffle mix

1 teaspoon vanilla extract

½ cup water, plus 2 tablespoons

12 Oreos or other chocolate sandwich cookies

1 tablespoon confectioners' sugar

1. Spray baking pan with oil or nonstick spray and place in basket.

2. Preheat air fryer to 390°F.

3. In a medium bowl, mix together the pancake mix, vanilla, and water.

4. Dip 4 cookies in batter and place in baking pan.

5. Cook for 6 minutes, until browned.

6. Repeat steps 4 and 5 for the remaining cookies.

7. Sift sugar over warm cookies.

> **VARIATION:** Try other flavors of sandwich cookies. For a wedding cake cookie, use Golden Oreos and substitute almond extract for the vanilla. In the fall, our local store stocks Pumpkin Spice cookies. If using those, add ¼ teaspoon pumpkin pie spice to the confectioners' sugar before sifting over cookies. The possibilities are almost endless!

Gingerbread

Yield: 1 loaf (approx. 6–8 servings) | Prep Time: 5 minutes | Cooking Time: 20 minutes | Total Time: 25 minutes

KID PLEASER   SUPER EASY   VEGETARIAN

Molasses contains nutrients such as iron, magnesium, calcium, and B vitamins. Blackstrap molasses is the most nutritious variety, but many people find it too bitter for gingerbread and other sweets. For best results, use unsulphured dark molasses.

cooking spray

1 cup flour

2 tablespoons sugar

3/4 teaspoon ground ginger

1/4 teaspoon cinnamon

1 teaspoon baking powder

1/2 teaspoon baking soda

1/8 teaspoon salt

1 egg

1/4 cup molasses

1/2 cup buttermilk

2 tablespoons oil

1 teaspoon pure vanilla extract

1. Preheat air fryer to 330°F.

2. Spray 6 x 6-inch baking dish lightly with cooking spray.

3. In a medium bowl, mix together all the dry ingredients.

4. In a separate bowl, beat the egg. Add molasses, buttermilk, oil, and vanilla and stir until well mixed.

5. Pour liquid mixture into dry ingredients and stir until well blended.

6. Pour batter into baking dish and cook at 330°F for 20 minutes or until toothpick inserted in center of loaf comes out clean.

Grilled Pineapple Dessert

Yield: 4 servings | Prep Time: 5 minutes | Cooking Time: 12 minutes | Total Time: 17 minutes

GLUTEN FREE   KID PLEASER   SUPER EASY   TASTER FAVORITE   VEGETARIAN

This dish works especially well on a grilling plate, which gives the pineapple slices nice grill marks and a little extra crisp. If you don't own a grill plate, just place your pineapple slices in the air fryer basket. The results will differ a little, but it won't disappoint!

---

oil for misting or cooking spray

4 ½-inch-thick slices fresh pineapple, core removed

1 tablespoon honey

¼ teaspoon brandy

2 tablespoons slivered almonds, toasted

vanilla frozen yogurt or coconut sorbet

1. Spray both sides of pineapple slices with oil or cooking spray. Place on grill plate or directly into air fryer basket.

2. Cook at 390°F for 6 minutes. Turn slices over and cook for an additional 6 minutes.

3. Mix together the honey and brandy.

4. Remove cooked pineapple slices from air fryer, sprinkle with toasted almonds, and drizzle with honey mixture.

5. Serve with a scoop of frozen yogurt or sorbet on the side.

Peach Cobbler

Yield: 4 servings | Prep Time: 15 minutes | Cooking Time: 12–14 minutes | Total Time: 27–29 minutes

KID PLEASER **VEGETARIAN**

America's all-time favorite dessert may be apple pie, but peach cobbler runs a very close second. Our version contains lots more fruit than crust and uses far less sugar than traditional recipes. It also makes only 4 servings, so you won't be tempted to binge.

---

16 ounces frozen peaches, thawed, with juice (do not drain)

6 tablespoons sugar

1 tablespoon cornstarch

1 tablespoon water

Crust

½ cup flour

¼ teaspoon salt

3 tablespoons butter

1½ tablespoons cold water

¼ teaspoon sugar

1. Place peaches, including juice, and sugar in air fryer baking pan. Stir to mix well.

2. In a small cup, dissolve cornstarch in the water. Stir into peaches.

3. In a medium bowl, combine the flour and salt. Cut in butter using knives or a pastry blender. Stir in the cold water to make a stiff dough.

4. On a floured board or wax paper, pat dough into a square or circle slightly smaller than your air fryer baking pan. Cut diagonally into 4 pieces.

5. Place dough pieces on top of peaches, leaving a tiny bit of space between the edges. Sprinkle very lightly with sugar, no more than about ¼ teaspoon.

6. Cook at 360°F for 12 to 14 minutes, until fruit bubbles and crust browns.

Strawberry Pastry Rolls

Yield: 4 servings | Prep Time: 20 minutes | Cooking Time: 5–6 minutes per batch | Total Time: 30–32 minutes

KID PLEASER VEGETARIAN

Phyllo dough may look intimidating, but it's extremely easy to use, and the air fryer cooks it to perfection. Instead of drenching it in butter, we've lightened it up by using butter-flavored cooking spray. See insert A3 for recipe photo.

---

3 ounces low-fat cream cheese

2 tablespoons plain yogurt

2 teaspoons sugar

1/4 teaspoon pure vanilla extract

8 ounces fresh strawberries

8 sheets phyllo dough

butter-flavored cooking spray

1/4–1/2 cup dark chocolate chips (optional)

1. In a medium bowl, combine the cream cheese, yogurt, sugar, and vanilla. Beat with hand mixer at high speed until smooth, about 1 minute.

2. Wash strawberries and destem. Chop enough of them to measure 1/2 cup. Stir into cheese mixture.

3. Preheat air fryer to 330°F.

4. Phyllo dough dries out quickly, so cover your stack of phyllo sheets with waxed paper and then place a damp dish towel on top of that. Remove only one sheet at a time as you work.

5. To create one pastry roll, lay out a single sheet of phyllo. Spray lightly with butter-flavored spray, top with a second sheet of phyllo, and spray the second sheet lightly.

6. Place a quarter of the filling (about 3 tablespoons) about 1/2 inch from the edge of one short side. Fold the end of the phyllo over the filling and keep rolling a turn or two. Fold in both the left and right sides so that the edges meet in the middle of your roll. Then roll up completely. Spray outside of pastry roll with butter spray.

7. When you have 4 rolls, place them in the air fryer basket, seam side down, leaving some space in between each. Cook at 330°F for 5 to 6 minutes, until they turn a delicate golden brown.

8. Repeat step 7 for remaining rolls.

9. Allow pastries to cool to room temperature.

10. When ready to serve, slice the remaining strawberries. If desired, melt the chocolate chips in microwave or double boiler. Place 1 pastry on each dessert plate, and top with sliced strawberries. Drizzle melted chocolate over strawberries and onto plate.

> **TIP:** Use a spoon or the tines of a fork to drizzle the chocolate. Another option is to transfer the melted chocolate into a small plastic bag. Snip off a tiny piece of the corner and squeeze out the chocolate as you would with a pastry bag.

Sweet Potato Donut Holes

Yield: 18 | Prep Time: 10 minutes | Cooking Time: 4–5 minutes per batch | Total Time: 18–20 minutes

KID PLEASER   SUPER EASY   VEGETARIAN

Purple sweet potatoes are low in fat and packed with antioxidants. They're also a good source of fiber, calcium, and iron. Your kids won't care about any of that, but they will love the color. Combining purple sweet potatoes with the other ingredients makes your cooked donut holes turn a beautiful, brilliant blue! When buying purple sweet potatoes, look for varieties grown locally and labeled non-GMO.

---

1 cup flour

1/3 cup sugar

1/4 teaspoon baking soda

1 teaspoon baking powder

1/8 teaspoon salt

1/2 cup cooked mashed purple sweet potatoes

1 egg, beaten

2 tablespoons butter, melted

1 teaspoon pure vanilla extract

oil for misting or cooking spray

1. Preheat air fryer to 390°F.

2. In a large bowl, stir together the flour, sugar, baking soda, baking powder, and salt.

3. In a separate bowl, combine the potatoes, egg, butter, and vanilla and mix well.

4. Add potato mixture to dry ingredients and stir into a soft dough.

5. Shape dough into 1½-inch balls. Mist lightly with oil or cooking spray.

6. Place 9 donut holes in air fryer basket, leaving a little space in between. Cook for 4 to 5 minutes, until done in center and lightly browned outside.

7. Repeat step 6 to cook remaining donut holes.

> **TIP:** We like these best as they are, but for a super-sweet treat you can add a very light dusting of confectioners' sugar.

Tortilla Fried Pies

Yield: 12 pies | Prep Time: 10 minutes | Cooking Time: 5 minutes per batch | Total Time: 20 minutes

SUPER EASY   TASTER FAVORITE   VEGETARIAN

We like making these with our own home-preserved figs, but you have plenty of other options. For a sugar-free dessert, choose one of the many widely available all-fruit spreads.

12 small flour tortillas (4-inch diameter)

½ cup fig preserves

¼ cup sliced almonds

2 tablespoons shredded, unsweetened coconut

oil for misting or cooking spray

1. Wrap refrigerated tortillas in damp paper towels and heat in microwave 30 seconds to warm.

2. Working with one tortilla at a time, place 2 teaspoons fig preserves, 1 teaspoon sliced almonds, and ½ teaspoon coconut in the center of each.

3. Moisten outer edges of tortilla all around.

4. Fold one side of tortilla over filling to make a half-moon shape and press down lightly on center. Using the tines of a fork, press down firmly on edges of tortilla to seal in filling.

5. Mist both sides with oil or cooking spray.

6. Place hand pies in air fryer basket close but not overlapping. It's fine to lean some against the sides and corners of the basket. You may need to cook in 2 batches.

7. Cook at 390°F for 5 minutes or until lightly browned. Serve hot.

8. Refrigerate any leftover pies in a closed container. To serve later, toss them back in the air fryer basket and cook for 2 or 3 minutes to reheat.

THIS & THAT

Air-Boiled Eggs

Yield: 4 eggs | Prep Time: 1 minute | Cooking Time: 9–13 minutes | Total Time: 10–14 minutes

GLUTEN FREE SUPER EASY VEGETARIAN

Yes, you can "boil" eggs in an air fryer! It won't save you any time, but this recipe might come in handy on a busy cooking day when you're using your entire range top for other dishes.

---

4 eggs

> **NOTE:** The exterior of the egg white may darken slightly during cooking. This doesn't affect taste, but you may not like the appearance for certain dishes. Test one out ahead of time to see for yourself.

1. Place eggs in air fryer basket and cook at 300°F for 9 minutes.
2. Your timing may vary slightly, but your eggs should be soft-cooked, with solid whites and still slightly runny yolks.
3. Cook 1 minute more for a slightly firmer yolk.
4. Cook 2 to 3 more minutes (for a total of 12 to 13 minutes) for hard-cooked eggs.

Garlic

Yield: 1 bulb | Prep Time: 5 minutes | Cooking Time: 15 minutes | Total Time: 20 minutes

GLUTEN FREE SUPER EASY VEGETARIAN

You can cook multiple bulbs at once but only as many bulbs as your air fryer will hold in a single layer.

---

1 bulb garlic
⅛ teaspoon extra-light virgin olive oil

> **TIP:** If you prefer to use more oil, cut a small piece of aluminum foil and form a little cup around the bottom of the garlic. This will hold the pod upright so the oil soaks into the cloves rather than dripping onto the bottom of your appliance.

1. Preheat air fryer to 360°F.
2. Cut off top of garlic bulb to expose clove tips.
3. Drizzle oil over top of clove tips.
4. Cook at 360°F for 15 minutes or until garlic softens and is roasted through.

Garlic Croutons

Yield: 2 cups | Prep Time: 10 minutes | Cooking Time: 6 minutes | Total Time: 16 minutes

SUPER EASY **VEGETARIAN**

Browning the butter adds a nice, rich taste to these croutons, but watch closely while you're heating the butter. It can burn very quickly.

---

1 tablespoon butter

1 tablespoon extra-light olive oil

½ teaspoon garlic powder

½ teaspoon dried parsley flakes

1 small loaf ciabatta bread, about 8 ounces (enough to make 4 cups of cubed bread)

1. In a small saucepan, heat butter on low just until it browns.

2. Stir in the oil, garlic powder, and parsley. Let sit while preparing bread.

3. Cut ciabatta bread into ¾-inch cubes. Place 4 cups of cubed bread into large bowl.

4. Drizzle butter and oil mixture over bread cubes and stir to coat well.

5. Cook at 390°F for 3 minutes. Stir and cook 3 minutes longer or until croutons are golden brown and crunchy all the way through.

VARIATION: Ciabatta or artisan bread will give you denser croutons. If you prefer light and airy croutons, use French bread instead.

Mini Peppers

Yield: 4–8 servings | Prep Time: 11 minutes | Cooking Time: 15 minutes | Total Time: 26 minutes

GLUTEN FREE   SUPER EASY   VEGETARIAN

These little red, orange, and yellow peppers taste great raw in a salad or stuffed with a filling. Roasting them brings out their natural sweetness, though, and enhances their flavor. Try them alongside our Italian Tuna Roast (page 126).

1-pound bag mixed mini peppers

1 tablespoon olive oil

1. Wash the peppers, split them into halves, and seed them.

2. Toss in oil to coat thoroughly.

3. Place in the air fryer basket and cook at 390°F for 5 minutes.

4. Shake basket to redistribute peppers and cook for 5 more minutes.

5. Shake basket again and cook for an additional 5 minutes. Peppers are done when some of the edges brown.

Nuts

Yield: 1 cup | Prep Time: 1 minute | Cooking Time: 5–7 minutes | Total Time: 6–8 minutes

GLUTEN FREE   SUPER EASY   VEGETARIAN

Total cooking time will vary because some nuts cook more quickly than others. Pause your air fryer after 3 minutes to check progress. If you need to cook longer, keep a close watch because nuts toast very quickly in an air fryer. Sometimes the difference between lightly toasted and dark roasted can be less than a minute!

1 cup blanched, whole almonds (or walnuts, pecans, or other nuts)

1. Preheat air fryer to 360°F.

2. Place whole almonds in air fryer basket.

3. Cook almonds for 3 minutes, stop, and shake the basket.

4. Continue cooking for 2 to 4 more minutes or until nuts brown to your liking.

> **TIP:** For best results, cook nuts in a single layer. Depending on the size of your air fryer basket, you may be able to roast more than 1 cup at a time.

Toast, Plain & Simple

Yield: 2 pieces | Prep Time: 1 minute | Cooking Time: 3–5 minutes | Total Time: 4–6 minutes

KID PLEASER   SUPER EASY   VEGETARIAN

Nothing could be simpler than plain toast. Sometimes there's nothing better than a slice with a cup of hot tea.

---

2 slices bread

1. Cut each bread slice in half (for a better fit).

2. Place in air fryer basket.

3. Cook at 360°F for 3 minutes. Turn and cook an additional 1 to 2 minutes, until both sides brown.

TIP: We tested different types of bread for toasting in the air fryer. Commercial oat nut bread toasted well, as did ordinary wheat and white sandwich bread. Other seeded and sprouted grain breads tended to cook unevenly.

JUST FOR FUN

Children and other people with picky palates are more open to trying new foods when they're fun, and we grown-ups like to play with our food too! After all, who doesn't love a picnic, even if inclement weather means having it indoors?

The meals that follow will make special days even more special and ordinary weeknight meals extraordinary. They each feed 4, but you can double them to feed more. They're meant to be easy and fun and help spark some ideas of your own. Add to or subtract from the ingredient lists as you like.

AZTEC SUPPER

This beautiful tray is also a great potluck contribution. For a large crowd, you might want to take two.

1 cup sour cream

2 large avocados

juice of 1 small lime

2 cups shredded Cheddar cheese

16-ounce jar salsa

3 cups shredded lettuce

1 bag triangle-shaped tortilla chips

Pinto Taquitos (page 142)

1. In the center of a round tray, spread the sour cream in a 6-inch circle.

2. Peel and dice the avocados and toss with the lime juice. Mound them on top of the sour cream.

3. Cover the avocados thickly with the shredded cheese.

4. Spoon the salsa around the circle.

5. Scatter the lettuce around the salsa.

6. Arrange the tortilla chips around the edge of the tray with points facing out. Lay the taquitos between the chips and the lettuce.

CHRISTMAS BREAKFAST

Here's a breakfast that doesn't need a knife or fork. Fill a bowl with clementines or other easy-to-peel citrus fruit. Linger over coffee and enjoy a relaxed morning watching the kids play.

Cheddar-Ham-Corn Muffins (page 5)

clementines, tangerines, or small oranges

figs, dates, plums, cherries, raisins, or other dried fruits

shelled nuts

small cheese crackers

granola bars (wrappers on)

1. Place the muffins on a plate or platter set on a table near the tree.

2. Pile the oranges in a bowl and arrange the granola bars, still in their wrappers, among the oranges.

3. Mix the dried fruit, nuts, and cheese crackers together in a pretty bowl and set everything on the table near the tree.

> NOTE: All you need is a napkin to catch the crumbs— and maybe an after-breakfast candy cane!

MEDITERRANEAN ANTIPASTI DINNER

This would make good use of leftover roast, although we often make the Italian Tuna Roast just for this special dinner.

Italian Tuna Roast (page 126)

1 box thin crisp breadsticks or 1 loaf French or Italian bread, torn into chunks

4 ounces small mozzarella balls or 4 ounces cubed Parmesan cheese

4 ounces mixed olives

1 small jar roasted red peppers

4–6 stuffed grape leaves

½ cup bite-size tomatoes, such as grape or cherry

2 cups melon cubes

biscotti or amaretti cookies

1. Break the tuna into large rough chunks and place in the center of a large platter.

2. Place the breadsticks in a large glass.

3. Drain the mozzarella balls, olives, and roasted red peppers.

4. Arrange prepared ingredients (except cookies) around the tuna. Each diner helps himself or herself.

5. For dessert, serve the cookies with small cups of hot, strong coffee.

MOROCCAN FEAST

Spread a colorful blanket or sheet on the floor and enjoy this meal picnic-style, or take it outside for even more fun. Cleanup is a breeze: no plates or silverware to wash.

Lamb Chops (page 99)

1 box couscous or saffron rice mix

1 or 2 single-serving bags green tea with mint per person

2 large oranges

cinnamon

6–8 stuffed grape leaves

8-ounce tub hummus

1 cup cucumber slices

1 cup carrot strips

4 pita breads

1. Double the Lamb Chops recipe.

2. While the lamb chops are cooking, cook the couscous or rice according to package directions.

3. Brew the tea according to package directions.

4. Slice the oranges and lightly sprinkle with cinnamon.

5. Mound the couscous or rice in the center of a large brightly colored platter.

6. Arrange the lamb chops on the couscous with the bones crossing a bit in the center.

7. Arrange all the other foods around them.

> **NOTE:** To eat, tear the pita bread in pieces and use them to scoop up the couscous or hummus. Dip the carrot strips and cucumber strips in the hummus as well. Eat the lamb chops with your fingers. Serve the tea in small, heat-proof glasses or cups and finish the meal with the orange slices.

PICNIC IN THE PARK

Pack a lunch and head for the park! Wrapping the sandwiches in foil and storing them in a warm insulated container will keep them fresh and delicious until you're ready to eat.

Sloppy Joes (page 110)

carrot sticks

bottled water

flavored yogurt in tubes or individual cups

veggie chips (or your chip of choice)

1. When the Sloppy Joes are nearly done, rinse a small insulated container with warm water.

2. Wrap each sandwich in two layers of aluminum foil and place in the container. If taking warm washcloths for cleaning up hands, place those in the chest too.

3. In another small container, pack the carrot sticks, bottled water, and yogurt. Add a sealable plastic bag of ice to keep everything cold.

4. Find a table or good spot and open everything up.

5. Enjoy the yogurt for dessert.

SPRING SPREAD

In the South, spring is the perfect time to eat outdoors. Temperatures are mild, and the sun feels so good after the dreary winter weather. Set up a table outside and invite three friends to join you for a luncheon at which you can catch up on all the latest news.

Salmon Salad with Steamboat Dressing (page 184)

1 pint fresh strawberries

1 small lemon

1 pint low-fat frozen vanilla yogurt or coconut sorbet

1 box whole-grain crackers

2 liters sparkling water, flavored or plain

2 ounces toasted coconut

4 cups coffee

1. Make the Salmon Salad and dressing and refrigerate.

2. Slice the strawberries and chill.

3. Cut the lemon in half lengthwise and slice into 8 half-moon slices.

4. Scoop the frozen yogurt or sorbet into 4 individual dishes and keep in the freezer until needed.

5. Set the table outside with a pretty tablecloth or printed bedsheet and your prettiest china and glassware.

6. Place the salad in the center of the table. Serve the dressing in a pretty dish with a spoon or small ladle and place a basket of crackers on the table.

7. Fill the glasses with ice-cold sparkling water and garnish each glass with 2 lemon slices.

8. For dessert, spoon the berries over the frozen yogurt and sprinkle with toasted coconut.

9. Finish with coffee and enjoy the lovely day.

APPENDIX A

CONVERSION CHART

Values in the table below are approximate. For the Fahrenheit temperatures used in this book, Celsius temperatures have been rounded. Temperature controls on air fryers differ, and you can adjust most in increments no smaller than 5 or 10 degrees.

Fahrenheit	Celsius
390	200
360	180
330	165
300	150
270	130
240	115
210	100
180	80
150	65

For precise calculations, see metric-conversions.org/temperature/celsius-to-fahrenheit.htm or check your preferred reference.

AIR FRYER BUYING GUIDE

As air fryers continue to grow in popularity, the market is flooding with choices. A few short years ago, the selection in the American market was very limited. Today, dozens of models are available from a wide range of manufacturers. Many brand names may be unfamiliar, while you may have known and loved others for years.

Even though you have a huge selection from which to choose, research isn't too difficult because air fryers aren't terribly complex machines. Let's begin with the two most important considerations: size and capacity.

Size

Air fryers are not small appliances. If you have very limited kitchen space, ask yourself whether you can or want to sacrifice room on your countertop. Look up the dimensions of the units you're considering and do some measuring in your kitchen. Don't forget to check the air fryer's height to make sure it will fit under overhanging cabinets.

Also factor ventilation into your decision. During operation, most air fryers need some open space both above and behind the unit. For details on a specific model, you usually can find the owner's manual online. If not, find the manufacturer's website and call or email them. If you can't

find either, you may want to consider a different manufacturer. More on that later.

Very high-fat foods, such as bacon and ground beef or lamb, may cause your air fryer to smoke. Sometimes you can solve the problem by adding a little water to the air fryer drawer. Coconut also tends to smoke a lot, but in that case water won't help. The best solution, especially for frequent users, is to place your air fryer next to your range so you can turn on the exhaust fan when needed. Excessive smoking is *not* normal, however, and may indicate that your appliance is malfunctioning. If that happens, unplug it immediately and contact the manufacturer.

Capacity

Most people who see an air fryer for the first time are surprised that the appliance is so large, and they are equally as surprised that the interior cooking capacity is so small. The original or regular size has a capacity of about 3.7 quarts. The extra-large size has a capacity of about 5.8 quarts.

All the recipes in this cookbook were designed for regular air fryers. This capacity is certainly suitable for singles and couples, but cooking for more than two people often requires cooking in batches. If you plan to use your air fryer a lot and for four or more people, consider going with the extra-large size.

Features

Whether you choose manual or digital controls is mainly a matter of personal preference. In our experience, neither has significant advantages over the other. Control panels on some models include presets, which allow you to select a preprogrammed time and temperature with the push of a single button. These presets can prove useful, but they aren't foolproof. Exact timing depends on many factors, such as amount of food, size of pieces, and temperature of food. For that reason, we're not fans of presets, but again, it's a matter of individual preference.

All air fryers have timers, but they all don't work the same. Some have a limit of 30 minutes. That's fine for most recipes, but large foods such as whole beets or a pork roast can take 40 minutes or longer to cook. Timers also can function differently. You often need to stop once or twice during cooking to shake the basket to redistribute foods for even cooking. Sometimes you'll want to check on food to prevent overcooking, especially if you're new to air frying. Most timers will pause when you stop or open the fryer and then continue from where they left off when you resume cooking. One older model had a timer that didn't allow for pausing. If you stopped the appliance during cooking, the timer instantly reset itself to zero. This model is no longer for sale, but it illustrates the value in investigating details before you buy.

Accessories

The most useful accessory for your air fryer is a baking dish. It allows you to cook foods with high liquid content, eggs, meats and vegetables with sauces, and even small casseroles. You also can use your pan to cook all sorts of baked goods, such as cakes, custards, and breads. Baking pans made for air fryers will fit snugly so the basket gives maximum cooking capacity. They also have a handle for easy removal. You can use other oven-safe dishes in an air fryer as long as they clear the heating element, but that handle makes a huge difference. To get the most enjoyment from your appliance, a good air fryer baking pan is well worth the investment.

Also consider a grill plate, which gives you a ribbed surface that's more solid than the wire mesh air fryer basket. It allows for a bit of a sear on the outsides of meat, poultry, or even pineapple slices. If you can buy only one accessory, make it the baking pan. If you can manage a second, get the grill plate.

Some air fryers include a double layer rack, which lets you cook more at once by stacking a second layer of food on the rack. It sounds like a good idea, but it has drawbacks. During cooking, you can't see the bottom layer of food to check for doneness. You have to remove the hot rack first, being careful not to let the food on top slide off, which can prove awkward. The top rack also sits very close to the top of the air fryer. That means that any food you place on that top rack must be fairly thin; otherwise it could come in direct contact with the heating element.

Manufacturer and Warranty

Regardless of whether you're familiar with a brand name, it pays to do your research. Fortunately, the Internet makes that easy. Before you buy an air fryer, find the manufacturer's website and look up warranty terms. Warranties on air fryers can range from two years to just 30 days, and they may cover only the unit itself, the various parts, or some combination.

The owner's manual often includes warranty information and usually is available online or by request from the company. Again, if you have difficulty obtaining information about the product or contacting the manufacturer, beware. It's a pretty sure bet that any company that isn't helpful before the sale isn't going to be more helpful after the sale.

Price

More often than not, you'll find much better prices if you don't buy directly from the manufacturer.

There's no reason to pay a premium price as long as you choose a reputable seller. Whether shopping locally or online, check the return policy and other terms before you buy. Even high-quality manufacturers produce a lemon every now and then, and sometimes products can sustain damage during shipping.

If you do experience a problem, you'll get faster results if you make the correct contact. When merchandise arrives damaged or you receive the wrong product, contact the seller immediately. The manufacturer most often will handle a warranty claim.

For information on specific air fryers, visit TheHealthyKitchenShop.com, which has comparison charts designed to provide a broad overview that will help you narrow your choices. You also can read detailed reviews containing all the latest information on the top-selling air fryer brands and models.

IMAGE CREDITS

INDEX